Remembering Willie

Remembering Willie

University Press of Mississippi / Jackson

First Edition

ISBN 1-57806-267-5

British Library Cataloging-in-Publication Data available

Photograph on page 112 © Kay Holloway

CONTENTS

NOTE FROM THE PUBLISHER

When Willie Morris died suddenly on 2 August 1999, we at the University Press of Mississippi grieved that we had lost a beloved author and friend.

To honor Willie's memory we have collected in this volume the eulogies given at his funeral on 5 August in Yazoo City, Mississippi, and some of the many tributes published in the days following his death.

We are grateful to the writers who generously agreed to have their words reprinted here. Each tribute in its own way captures the spirit of one of America's great writers and benevolent souls.

Remembering Willie

REVEREND WILL D. CAMPBELL

Somewhere up with the wind, Willie, you're finally free. Somewhere up with the wind, but you'll never be far away.

Willie Morris. Let us softly speak his name and move on. Let us shed a silent tear . . . and move on.

We don't know much about the hereafter. Or certainly I don't. But of one thing we can be certain, there are some questions being raised up there this afternoon. Disputation about how things are run that side of the Great Divide; suggestions along the way. Willie was never one to accept something just because that was the way it had always been done. And authority was something to be controverted, not conceded without contention. So perhaps if we listen: "Away with your silly harps. Where's Mamma and her pipe organ? And where's Jim Jones? And Truman? And Irwin? And Mr. Bill . . . get him over here. Let's get this place organized. Get us some 4 x 6 cards. And a typewriter. We have to do a story about all this."

Willie did not make the Biblically allotted three-score-years-and-ten. But sweetness of the visit is not measured in terms of its longevity. So we mourn.

We cannot say that he belonged to us. Nothing that has life belongs to another. It comes as a gift, a matter of grace, and when it is gone, with all our technology and medical knowhow, we cannot preserve it. But we know that relationships no more end with farewell than does life end with what the clinicians call death. Yet what they call death has a nasty sting, a hurt with which we have to struggle to deal and recover.

We quarrel with the Creator. What He so freely gave us, we do now grudgingly return. But without apology for the grudge. For that is what distinguishes the finite from the infinite—mortals from Almighty God.

I cannot sum up his years amongst us in these few minutes. So as we let him go . . . and we must now . . . let him go. . . . As we do, each of you must write your own words of eulogy and epitaph, in your own way, upon your own heart, and based on your own memories.

He was father, spouse, friend, colleague, and neighbor. He meant many and different things to all of us. Willie was a lot of things. Oh, but we must be judicious in our usage of the verb. Not *was*. *Is*. For what he was, he is, only now more so. That is our faith. His sense of justice is now a perfected reality, his struggle for equality across racial, religious, ethnic, class, and economic lines has reached fruition. His books upon which we thought there was no room for improvement are now edited to perfection. For, yes, you can take it with you. And you can keep it forever.

Letting him go means going back into the world. Soon it will be time for you who mourn to do that. It is a bitter pill. We who stand with you now cannot camouflage the gall nor shoulder your burden. We can but say that Willie is now in better hands than ours. We can also say that as you go back into the world, we are going with you. For we are your people.

And as we let him go we ask of this sweet soul, this big man–little boy combo, this simple and complex genius, this literary giant whose likeness we are not apt to see again . . . , of him who gave so very much of himself to us, we ask one last request. Save for us, at our last, old pal, some yarns to spin, some phrases to turn, new words to learn, a place at your table with a glass of something fine of the grape, and give us a big Willie Morris belly laugh to welcome us home.

Willie Morris. Let us softly speak his name and move on.

AMEN

WILLIAM STYRON

Willie left us much too soon. It seems inconceivable to me that now, after our friendship of nearly thirty-five years, I won't be hearing that soft voice calling me from Jackson, Mississippi, on the telephone. For many years he'd addressed me by the name of the narrator of one of my novels. "Stingo," I'd hear him say, "this is Willie. Are you in good spirits?" When I'd tell him I was or wasn't, or was somewhere in between, he'd then ask the next most urgent question. For Willie the creatures in God's scheme of things that ranked right next to people in importance were dogs, and he would ask about my golden retriever and black Lab. "How is Tashmoo? And how is Dinah? Give them all my love." Now that impish and tender voice is gone forever.

In 1965, before I ever met him, Willie extracted from me a long article for the issue of *Harper's* commemorating the end of the Civil War. Shortly after this I first laid eyes on Willie in the office at Yale University of the South's greatest historian, C. Vann Woodward, from whom Willie had also enticed an essay for that issue. That afternoon I drove Willie into New York City, and we got so passionately engrossed in conversation, as southerners often do when they first meet, about places and historical events and ancestral connections—in particular, our stumbling upon the realization that my North Carolina-born great-great-uncle had been state treasurer of Mississippi when Willie's great-great-grandfather was governor—we got so hypnotically involved in such talk that I missed the correct toll booth at the Triborough Bridge and drove far into Long Island before the error dawned.

I can't imagine a more glorious time for writers and journalists than the frenzied last years of the '60s when Willie, a mere kid, was guiding *Harper's* magazine with such consummate skill and imagination, summoning the finest writing talents in America to describe and interpret an unprecedented scene of social upheaval, with the war in Vietnam and racial strife threatening to blow the country apart. In the pages of his magazine Willie orchestrated these themes—and subthemes like the sexual revolution—with the wise aplomb of an editorial master, and for several golden years his creation was the preeminent journal in the nation, not only its keenest observer of political and social affairs but its most attractive literary showcase.

I was a night person in those days, and Willie too was nocturnal, and I think it was partly our mutual restlessness—two excited southern night-owls on the prowl in the Big Cave, as he called New York City—that cemented our friendship. We also spent countless evenings together in one or another of our homes in the country north of the city. Needless to say, we shared a great deal of strong drink, which helped us know each other better. What I came to know about Willie, among other things, was that animate and profound southernness was the energizing force in his life and what made him tick. Not that he was a professional southerner—he despised the obvious Dixieland clichés—and he got along well with Yankees; he had a richly and often humorously symbiotic relationship with New York Jewish intellectuals, many of whom admired him as much as he did them. It was just that he felt more at home with southerners, with whom he could share tall tales and indigenous jokes and family anecdotes and hilarious yarns that only the South can provide and that perhaps only expatriate southerners can enjoy in their cloying and sometimes desperate homesickness. Even then I had very little doubt that someday Willie would return home to Mississippi.

As I got to know Willie and became a close and devoted friend, I learned certain immutable things about him. I learned that he was unshakably loyal, that he was amazingly punctual about birthdays and commemorations and anniversaries of sorts, that he drank past healthy limits and that booze sometimes made him maudlin but never mean, that he was wickedly funny, that his country-boy openheartedness and candor masked an encyclopedic knowledge and an elegantly furnished mind, that he was moody and had a streak of dark paranoia that usually evaporated on a comic note, that he was an inveterate trickster and anecdotalist of practical jokes, that his furiously driven literary imagination allowed him to produce several unostentatious masterworks; that in him, finally, there was an essential nobility of spirit—no one ever possessed such a ready and ungrudging heart.

One of Willie's obsessions, aside from dogs, was graveyards. We went to many a burial ground together, from Appomattox to Shiloh. Once, on one of the many visits to Mississippi, he drove me out to a country cemetery some miles from Oxford. We had a few drinks and after a while he took me for a stroll among the headstones. Then, lo and behold, we spied an open book, a novel, propped against a grave marker. It took me a minute to realize that Willie had planted there my first novel, open to its epigraph from Sir Thomas Browne:

> *And since death must be the Lucina of life . . . since the brother of death daily haunts us with dying mementos . . . since our longest sun sets at right descencions, and makes but winter arches, and therefore it cannot be long before we lie down in darkness and have our light in ashes. . . .*

He was obviously delighted at my surprise. For Willie, a son of the South and from the town of Yazoo, death was fitting, in its place and season, as life—the life in which he achieved so much and gained such glory.

DAVID HALBERSTAM

We, who were his writers, loved Willie: no one ever did it better, no one made it more fun, and no one did it with greater sweetness. We understood, I think, that he was more than just a gifted writer and editor come to us from a distant place. I think we understood in some intuitive way that he was an ambassador from a new Mississippi, one that did not yet exist, but one day surely would—and that in the meantime he was a representative of a pained, troubled society which sent its most talented sons and daughters into momentary exile.

First, a few stories. The little boy in Willie always lived. He loved—like life itself—the telephone and playing telephone pranks. I always thought it was one of the great tragedies that the cell phone came into popular being so late in his life—had it come into existence a little earlier he would have been able to make so many more trick calls—and there could have been so many more Willies—Willie the Oxford Don, Willie the cool black disc jockey, Willie playing a redneck racist.

Let me tell you of one or two of the phone stories as we sit here remembering him. One of my favorite ones took place in January 1973. *The Best and the Brightest* had just come up and, to the delight of the author and the surprise of his publisher, had gone soaring up the *New York Times* bestseller list. After several weeks it was blessedly number one. What a marvelous moment! And then a dark cloud appeared. A book by a man named Dr. Robert Atkins, called *Robert Atkins' Diet Revolution* began to go surging up the charts. I still have my doubts about it as a diet book. As I recall it allowed you to eat as much as you wanted, particularly fatty foods, and yet you would somehow become slimmer—the fat according to Dr. Atkins, as I recall it, would devour itself. I suppose that makes it the perfect American late century diet book. Watching it rise was bad enough, but soon true tragedy struck. *Dr. Atkins passed me on the bestseller list*: he was number one and I was number two. And then one day the phone rang.

And there was the voice which sounded like an Oxford Don, and it belonged to a man who said that he was Dr. Robert Atkins and that he had noticed that both our books were on the bestseller list. Of course, he noted, he had just passed me. But he said, he thought we could collaborate on a new book, and with our special talents that book would surely be the biggest bestseller of all time. I was surely, he quickly added, too big a man to let his ascendance over me stand in our way. We could call it, he said, "The Best and the Fattest."

"I know that's you, Willie Weeks Morris," I said. And he giggled with a little boy's pleasure.

Or the day that Bob Kotlowitz, our managing editor, came in and was told to call Leonard Bernstein, and do it immediately. And there on his desk was Bernstein's phone number. Only it wasn't the Leonard Bernstein who was the great composer-conductor, it was Leonard Bernstein who was a Manhattan dentist. And Bob called and said that he had been told to call, that he had urgent need to talk to Leonard Bernstein. And Leonard Bernstein, the dentist, kept saying, "Are you in pain? Are you in pain?" and Bob, quickly catching on, said, "I'm always in pain."

Willie was a great editor with impeccable taste. He had marvelous instincts for what was happening in the country, and he always knew whom he wanted in the magazine. He always knew which writers to go to—and he knew that the only important thing was to get them to write about whatever it was that excited them. That would produce their best work.

That meant he was working all the time, and in effect he took his office with him.

Let me give you an example. One day he was at a cocktail party and he walked into Norman Mailer and he asked Mailer what he was up to, and Mailer said he was going to a Vietnam protest march at the Pentagon. "And you're going to write about it for *Harper's*," Willie quickly said, and Norman agreed. So they settled on 10,000 words for $10,000. And Mailer went out and soon the piece came back, only it was *100,000* words long. It was an editor's nightmare—or the nightmare for any other editor. Almost any other editor would have looked at it and tried to carve out the 15,000 best words and let it go at that. But Willie knew this was something important, one of America's very best and most impassioned writers on the subject that most excited him; a subject, by the way, which dominated the American agenda. It was Mailer doing what is arguably his best writing ever. And so he ran all of it. *All of it.* It was called *The Armies of the Night*, and in time it won the Pulitzer Prize.

That was the way Willie operated. My friend, Frank Conroy, who wrote the great book *Stop-Time*, told me the other night of running into Willie at Elaine's, a restaurant which served in those days as Willie's late-night office. It was 1969, just after the Manson murders.

"Who's covering the Manson murders for you?" Frank asked. "You are," Willie answered, and so that night around midnight Willie drew up a contract—on an Elaine's napkin, with Elio, the headwaiter, as witness—$10,000 for the piece. A very good article it was too.

And finally before I leave you today, as we bid farewell to this beloved man, I would like to talk about Willie's larger purpose, for it would be wrong to think of him only as a good old boy having a wonderful time in what he called the Big Cave—that was his name for Manhattan.

There was a purpose to everything Willie did, and the pursuit of that purpose was often painful, for it meant going up against his own people, the people he knew best and loved the most.

For he loved good writing and good books, but what he loved best was this region and this country. And he wanted the country to be made whole, and he knew that that could not happen until this most troubled part of the country entered a modern age. He knew all too well that the special American burden was race, the terrible legacy of slavery, and he knew as well that that burden weighed—if only in difference of degree—on the rest of the country as well. He knew that Mississippi could not be whole until it began to deal with race. And he knew that as long as America had a region that practiced its own form of apartheid, it would not be whole either. So behind all the charm and all the jokes, the Huck Finn exterior, that better America was the driving purpose of his life.

Race was always on his mind. It was one of our great bonds. This, if you will permit me a personal moment, is not the first time I have been to Yazoo City. The first time was in the fall of 1955, which was Willie's senior year in college. It was a few months after *Brown v. Board of Education*, and about thirty Yazoo blacks had signed a petition for school integration— and the White Citizens' Council had cracked down hard on them, and all but one or two had lost their jobs, and some of them had had their home mortgages placed in jeopardy.

And I came over here as a fledgling magazine writer for *The Reporter Magazine*—I was all of twenty-one. I was smuggled in by a young NAACP official named Medgar Evers (his brother Charles is here in the church today)—I felt I was part of some CIA high-risk affair, parachuting behind enemy lines. Three times I was moved from one car to another, always hidden in the back of the car, and driven door-to-door to talk to the people who had lost their jobs. I was scared to death that day—it's nice to return and not be scared. It's a piece of reporting I'm still proud of; Willie, still at Texas, read it, and it became the special link between Willie and me—I knew where he came from, and I knew something about his beloved hometown. That meant I knew something very important about Willie—that he hated the fact that the people whom he knew and loved best, the white people of his native state, did what they did to the other people he knew and loved best—the black people of Mississippi.

And so today seated as we are in this church in this town that Willie never really left, for he was about the most rooted man I ever knew, it seems to me that it has all come full circle for Willie. Willie began his professional life in New York in exile, and today he lay in state in the capitol in Jackson. He'd have loved that: I can remember him saying with the sweet pleasure of the innocent when we were younger, "Dave, I'm the youngest editor of *Harper's* magazine in its history," and I can hear him saying, "Dave, I lay there in state and only J. P. Coleman and John Stennis were honored that way in this century—how do you like those apples, Jim Eastland!"

And here on the podium along with that same boy who was so scared when he came here forty-four years ago to write about those people who lost their jobs are Will Campbell, who was ousted from his job as Ole Miss chaplain in 1956 and is one of the great heroes of the Civil Rights movement; and Bill Winter, the most elegant Southern politician of recent years; and Mike Espy, whose election meant so much to Willie. And all of it a sign, as Willie would have understood better than any of us, of how far we have come, and also how far we still have to go.

MIKE ESPY

Giving honor to God. To JoAnne, to the Morris family, and to all who are gathered here to celebrate the life of this marvelous man. I am honored to have been asked to offer brief reflections regarding my experiences while in the company of my friend, my "Yazoo buddy," Willie Morris.

I'll never forget the last time that I saw and talked with him. Of all the times this perhaps was indeed the most memorable for me. It was just after the local screening of *Ghosts of Mississippi*, about the murder of Medgar Evers and the trial of his assassin. Willie called and asked me to meet him at Crechale's, off Highway 80 in west Jackson. I tried to beg off; after all, this was 1996, and I was in the throes of some personal troubles. I told Willie that I had to deal with some "ghosts" of my own. But he insisted; he said that a good meal would make me feel better. He said that he wanted me to "see something." He wanted me to meet Rob Reiner and Alec Baldwin.

So reluctantly I turned my car toward the west Jackson restaurant, and I am so glad that I did. We hoisted glasses into the night. Libations of every type and kind. We consumed oily red Gulf snapper and fried onion rings. The talk was of movies, books, politics, and favorite places.

And I watched him talk and was reminded again of his abundant love of this place. Of what he has often called that certain "driftlessness," which characterizes this region's mood and movement. I listened as he described those subtle southern rhythms that he has chronicled so well in many books and stories. As he talked, I began to see what I think he wanted me to see. That is, in fact, how to change an attitude. How to disarm a predisposition.

He wanted the Hollywood types to know that "driftlessness" is not synonymous with "backwardness." That amiability does not necessarily make one less competitive. That folks down here can come off the porch and compete with the best of them and perform excellently in most any venue. In code that only colleagues can appreciate, he let them know that caricatures only go so far—that *this* South is changing—and can't forever be captured and encased within a celluloid frame.

He is—and will forever be—our region's greatest ambassador. Our avuncular bridge spanning the chasm from then to now.

He had differences that just work together. Degree by Oxford. Pedigree by Yazoo. Appreciated by literary houses. Welcome in juke joints. Well versed in the strictures of old segregation. But well able to lead others toward a more permanent inclusion. Willie Morris. Such an easy, likeable countenance. But so zealous for a proper understanding of this, our place.

There is an old Negro spiritual that I like, entitled "Let the Work I've Done Speak for Me." No need for persuasive oratory here. His works, thoughts, ideals have been set down for all time.

We today praise the life of this marvelous man. We remember and revere him for that agile mind, generous spirit, for those adventurous wanderings. And we respect him for his fierce loyalty to a place and to its people. We will certainly miss Willie Morris. He spoke *to* us. He spoke *for* us. Thank you.

JOSEPHINE AYRES HAXTON
(ELLEN DOUGLAS)

My very first memory of Willie is of his signing books—*North Toward Home*—at the McCormick Book Inn in Greenville. He was having a grand time and he made it an exciting time for everyone, and that's my overriding memory of him in his life—having a grand time and making it exciting for everyone.

The telephone might ring and a solemn-voiced official would be explaining that you'd violated a city ordinance against littering and must appear in court tomorrow. Ten o'clock sharp. Be there!

Willie! I know it's you!

Or one of the famous menus for his dinner parties: Vichyssoise Hushpuckena. But there was someone else, too, of course: the Willie who loved place names—Issaquena, Itta Bena, Mound Bayou, Midnight, Panther Burn, Savage, Pentecoste—and the eloquent Willie who wrote of "the Delta, relentless and abiding" "where the people played seven card stud against God." He brooded deeply and wrote courageously about our state—its beauty and cruelty and endlessly fascinating politics.

Willie cared for everything and everyone. His passion for football produced that remarkable book, *The Courting of Marcus Dupree*. His love of dogs and cats, the playful histories of his pets. People say if you love animals, you love them instead of loving people, but Willie's heart was big enough for both. He cared about his family, his friends, his colleagues, and he cared about the lives of the waiter at the Mayflower and the lady behind the cash register at the Jitney.

When I think of Willie I think of Huck Finn and Tom Sawyer. He had Huck's humanity and toughness of spirit and Tom's love of a joke—and of course an incisive intelligence that, like Twain's, recognized and grieved for the tragedies of his state and his country.

Like Huck and Tom, though, I know he'd like to be here, now, at his own funeral, ready to raise a glass with all his friends and relatives—to celebrate together.

GOVERNOR WILLIAM F. WINTER

If Willie Morris should hear about all of this carrying on over him here in Yazoo City today, I have the feeling that he might think that we were being a mite too serious. I know that he would revel in this gathering of so many of his old friends, but above all else he would want to be sure that everybody was having a good time.

So today in his passing, as in his living, all of us who were his friends find ourselves marveling at his intellectual and literary genius, even as we could never be in awe of him simply because he would not let us. Now, as we reflect on the magnitude of Willie's contributions to the world's literature, I find myself remembering him not so much for his international fame as for the fact that he was my warm and gracious neighbor, who let my grandchildren play in his backyard and who arranged for his cat, Spit McGee, to send my dog, Fritz, packages of dog biscuits.

For those of us who, like Willie, were, to use his word, ineffably affected by growing up in a Mississippi of myths and legends, of fantasy about what never was and hope for what might never be, of insufferable baseness and incredible goodness, he was the one who perhaps more than anybody else of our generation caused us to look within ourselves and discover there the joy and inspiration to sustain us through the good times and the bad.

I know that was true for me back in the late 1960s when I first heard about Willie Morris and when I was looking desperately for some voices that would speak of what I thought the South was really about—of civility and courtesy and kindness and tolerance—not of rage and hate and bitterness and bigotry. I found in his writings the special insight of one whose affection for his home state was not only undiminished but reenforced by his recognition of our weaknesses as well as our strengths and especially of our need to reach out to more, indeed to all, of our neighbors and to erase the barriers that separated us from one another.

There was no meanness and there was no pretense in Willie Morris. While not a publicly religious man, his life personified what true religion is all about. He found it not in the usual places but in the places where his friends were—in his words "at the ballgames and bus stations and courthouses and the bargain rate beauty parlors and the little churches and the roadhouses and the joints near closing time."

Willie found goodness and kindness in people wherever he met them. As an old Mississippi farmer said, "He didn't cull nobody."

And so on this day when we say good-bye to this good friend, let us be thankful that he passed this way and that we were fortunate enough to be with him on a brief part of his epic and unforgettable journey.

HARRIET DeCELL KUYKENDALL

I taught Willie algebra in high school.

He always said he liked me better than algebra, and I knew that to be the gospel truth—mainly because I never asked Willie to do something for me that he didn't do, except of course hand in all his algebra homework.

Willie made talks for me at groups I belong to and plan programs for. After a St. Andrew's Episcopal School Writers Workshop, where I had prevailed him to be the keynote speaker and scheduled him first off in the morning and insisted he be there *on time*, he said, "Harriet, don't *ever* again ask me to do something like this *so early in the morning*." And I didn't because Willie was a night person, as we all know.

I like to think I had a little bit to do with JoAnne and Willie's fortuitous marriage. Some of their early contacts were the result of those favors Willie was doing for me. He wrote the introduction to the history book JoAnne and I wrote about Yazoo County.

My students won a big prize from the Columbia Scholastic Press Association. JoAnne and I and seven students went to New York to receive the prize. Willie arranged a high tea at a wonderful Upper East Side apartment for the students, then invited JoAnne and me to a late dinner at Elaine's. (He invited an editor from Doubleday to the group, and I watched JoAnne captivate the editor. Then I watched Willie watching JoAnne captivate the editor.)

I was perhaps most grateful for what Willie said at my first husband Herman DeCell's funeral. Their friendship was based upon a very deep respect for each other's abilities.

Willie was the headliner in our National Library Week celebration in 1967, just before he became editor at *Harper's*. We liked to say that New Orleans had Mardi Gras, but Yazoo had National Library Week.

Willie brought an entourage along with him, friends from New York and Texas. Willie's old friend and basketball coach "Hardwood" Kelly, now superintendent of the school, had recently decreed over much opposition from the student body that no boy could have hair below the ear. Willie introduced his friend, Larry L. King, who rose to a standing ovation from the 800 students, his great red beard and collar length hair the same color as Kelly's face on the stage.

Willie insisted that he must talk at the all-black high school, ND Taylor, if he spoke at the all-white high school. I think such actions helped Yazoo get over the integration hurdle three years later.

One town comment went, "Willie is passing out Ralph Ellison's *Invisible Man* like calling cards." A few years later Willie was able to get some of us much sought-after tickets to an Ellison lecture and very small, private party in Jackson where we were able to really talk with Ellison. The friendship between the two was very apparent.

The reaction of the Yazooans to *North Toward Home* was very interesting. A self-conscious disbelief was prevalent: "Willie couldn't have done that, because I never did that." As if all our experiences were cloned. Yazoo's "tunnel vision" was opened a bit—the beginning of a much greater sophistication.

Some people resented his description of his parents. They called it "criticizing." They were very different people, and Willie loved each of them but in a different way. His perception helped me to see that my parents, too, were different, and I saw my attitude toward their memory was enlarged by Willie.

I think this quality of helping us to understand ourselves, our Southland, our relationships with others and to the larger world is the core of the appeal of Willie's books. He helps us realize our potential as well as our foibles. He calls us to be better than we are.

When JoAnne called me to participate today, knowing my eloquence could not match Willie's, I picked *his* words to read to you.

I think they are appropriate. I think Willie would approve. I read from my first edition of *North Toward Home.*

> [Harriet reads from page 31, "We took also to spending long hours in the cemetery . . . " to page 33, "On the days we would come and play until late afternoon, until the lightning-bugs came out and the crickets started making their chirping noises."]

JILL CONNER BROWNE

Willie was so fond of saying this—I cannot let this day pass without saying it—he would surely say it himself—"There hasn't been so much talent in one place since Thomas Jefferson died at Monticello . . . alone." And looking around here today, there certainly are a lot of talented people here, a lot of famous ones too. And Willie would love that. But the truth is, most of us here, don't nobody know who we are except us . . . and Willie. Willie knew and loved us all. And Lord, we loved him. So, I would have to amend Willie's saying to, "There hasn't been so much love in one place since, well, since the last time Willie had us all together over at his house."

Willie Morris had a remarkable effect on people. I first identified it by observing my daughter Bailey with him. She is very, very shy. But not with Willie. He brought out the best in her. It took about two seconds in that train of thought to see that he did the same thing for all of us. We knew—on a cellular level—how special he was. When dogs, cats, and children are instinctively drawn to a guy, the rest of us can feel pretty safe in following suit. Knowing how special he was made us feel better about ourselves, because he gave us his time and attention.

We have all been given the most amazing gift. But, if God had told us, Ok, I'm going to give you something wonderful. I am going to put this man in your life. And he is going to be your husband, your father, your friend, your mentor, and he will be the truest and the sweetest. He will be so sweet and so full of light, I will pretty much just set him down in some corner of some room of your life, and you will all be like a bunch of moths to his flame. You will stay up far too late, far too many nights, just to have a little while longer with his light and warmth. But on August 2, 1999, that flame will go out, and it will be very cold and very dark without it. If God had actually spoken those words to any one of us, every one of us would have willingly, happily, gratefully chosen this moment of cold dark misery, in order to have had every single possible moment in the warmth and brilliant light of the love of Willie Morris.

And when we realize that choice, we can look inward and know and see and feel that Willie left some of that flame inside each of us when he left—and it's just as warm and just as bright.

And that being so, all we can finally say is—Thank you, Willie . . . And thank you, God . . . amen.

WINSTON F. GROOM

Much has been said today about Willie's fascination with death and all its implications. He wasn't, of course, macabre about it; I think Willie felt it was simply the last defining moment and should be embraced with dignity. But his other favorite subject was baseball, and I remember on one occasion, by some coincidental circumstances, these two matters became intertwined for him.

This was back in the 1970s with the release of a movie called *Bang the Drum Slowly* starring Robert De Niro. It was about a minor league catcher who was dying, and I think Willie had seen it about ten times. I had not, and he was so determined that I should understand the impact of this movie that he took to acting it out. For instance, he would slide into "home" on a big Persian rug in my place and, having done so, would declare: "But he was a catcher, and he was dying!" In fact, Willie performed this sliding into home so many times that he actually slid a rut into my rug, which can still be seen today, and I have it as a souvenir to his memory.

A day ago I called our good mutual friend Adam Shaw to tell him about Willie. When he found out I was speaking here today, he asked what I was going to say. I told him I didn't know, and Adam said, "Well, why don't you thank him?" I thought about that for a few moments, and it seemed like the best idea I'd heard in a while. And so, finally, and I hope it's not too late, Thank you, Willie, for all your generosity to all the younger writers you helped—some of us not so young anymore—for all the time and energy and genuine caring for the written word and encouragement and efforts to make the unworkable work. It is a debt that can never be repaid. Thank you.

Of course, Willie had his quirks. He was a man of great humor and did not dislike many things, but there were a few. You all know about his positive dislike of telephones. And there was something else, too, that would draw his ire. This was when some literary critic decided he did not like something Willie had written, and I remember well one long luncheon afternoon in Bridgehampton many years ago when, after a long blustery tirade, Willie drew himself up and made the famous declaration: "I am not sure what people will be reading five hundred years from now, but I will guarantee you it will not be the 'Collected Reviews of Christopher Lehmann-Haupt'!" Willie also had a wonderful propensity to immediately make friends with people. Back when he was doing a stint as writer-in-residence for the *Washington Star*, he was living over in Alexandria, Virginia. Willie was a nocturnal person, of course, and many times around midnight, he'd get the munchies. There was, close to his place and mine, an all-night burger joint called the Little Tavern, and Willie would often go there and get a bag of burgers. One time he met a guy there and they got to talking and became friends and Willie decided nothing would do but to bring this man over to my place and introduce me to him. This was about 2 a.m. Imagine my astonishment when I was rousted out of bed and opened the door to find ole Willie standing there with none other than the famous Washington Redskins quarterback Sonny Jurgenson!

And, so, here we are, and like the song says, "It's a hot and dusty Delta Day." The great long journey, the great experience here, is over. But your friends and family are all here with you, Willie, just like you would have wanted and just like you knew they'd be!

Godspeed.

PETER APPLEBOME

Willie Morris, the writer and editor whose life and work reveled in the endless contradictions of the South and the region's ghostlike hold on its native sons and daughters, died on Monday at St. Dominic Hospital in Jackson, Mississippi, at sixty-four.

The cause was heart failure, said a hospital official.

Mr. Morris, who turned his childhood in Yazoo City, Mississippi, into a place almost as complex, resonant, and magical as William Faulkner's Yoknapatawpha County, went from a country boy to a Rhodes Scholar to a literary Wunderkind, becoming editor-in-chief of *Harper's* magazine at age thirty-two.

But just as Truman Capote famously said that all southerners eventually come home, if only in a box, Mr. Morris returned to Mississippi in 1980 and never stopped exploring what he once described as "the old warring impulses of one's sensibility to be both Southern and American."

He wrote on subjects ranging from his childhood English fox terrier to Mississippi race relations: hunkered down in his favorite Mississippi haunts like Doe's in Greenville, Lusko's in Greenwood and Bill's Greek Tavern in Jackson, and delved into the interplay of past and present in the South.

Still, rather than merely a vivid interpreter of southern life, Mr. Morris's legacy is as someone who was ahead of his time in exploring the confluence of region and nation, and how much the South's distinctive experience of race, family, and history was so deeply a part of the nation's experience as well.

"Willie said that Mississippi is America writ large," said Richard Howorth, owner of Square Books, the literary haunt in Oxford, Mississippi. "And to understand Willie you have to know that he had this amazing knowledge of American history. And I think his understanding of the South and curiosity about the South was very much a part of his understanding and curiosity about America. He understood the South as only a southerner could, but his perspective was so much broader than just thinking and writing about the South."

Willie Morris was born on November 29, 1934, in Jackson. When he was six his family moved to Yazoo City, a town on the edge of the Mississippi Delta, which at roughly the same time nurtured figures as diverse as Mike Espy, later to become Mississippi's first black congressman since Reconstruction and then secretary of agriculture; Haley Barbour, former national chairman of the Republican Party; and Zig Ziglar, the motivational speaker.

His father, Henry, ran a gas station, and Mr. Morris grew up at the tail end of the segregation era, in an environment he came to see as wondrous and horrific, where blacks and whites lived together in parallel universes that were apart and entwined. He played taps for the American Legion at military funerals, became a part-time sportswriter for the *Yazoo Herald*, and dreamed of ascending to the landed gentry who defined the social and economic overclass of the Delta.

But rather than send Mr. Morris to the University of Mississippi, his father had him go to the distant and alien environs of the University of Texas in Austin. He had, he later observed, no sense that "there were ideas, much less ideas to arouse one from oneself." But, after two years of pranks and fraternity hi-jinks, he came to see that books could be, as he later put it, "as subversive as Socrates." He became editor of the student newspaper, *The Daily Texan,* and later became a Rhodes Scholar and returned to Texas to edit *The Texas Observer.*

He moved to California and then to New York, where he was hired at *Harper's* magazine in 1963. In 1967 he became its youngest editor-in-chief ever. He presided over one of the legendary eras in magazine journalism, hiring David Halberstam to write about Vietnam, Larry L. King to write about Washington, and printing a 45,000-word excerpt of William Styron's *Confessions of Nat Turner* and 90,000 words of Norman Mailer's "Steps of the Pentagon" about a Vietnam War protest march, which took up the entire March 1968 issue. Six months after becoming editor-in-chief he also published his autobiography, *North Toward Home,* which was a memoir as social history that tried to make sense of the epic changes rattling through the South and what they said about the nation.

But after new ownership took over the magazine, Mr. Morris found himself at war with the management and resigned in 1971, and most of his staff followed.

Mr. Morris lived and wrote for several years from Bridgehampton, New York.

But in 1980 he returned home as writer-in-residence at the University of Mississippi. He moved ten years later to Jackson and spent his time evoking the clattering cacophony of warring emotions—love, hate, chauvinism, despair, and, above all, a sense of something unshakable—that so many southerners feel toward the region.

Not all of his work was critically praised. A 1973 novel, *The Last of the Southern Girls,* received tepid reviews. And his memoir of his days at *Harper's, New York Days,* struck some reviewers as conventional and nostalgic. But few doubt that he captured the South's transition from the days of segregation and the complexities of the southern experience like few, if any, writers of his time.

"His work in *North Toward Home* became a mantra for southerners who fled the South seeking worlds where they could be free and open in their thought but could never escape the love-hate relationship all southerners carry within them about the place of birth," said William R. Ferris, chairman of the National Endowment for the Humanities, and a long-time friend from Mississippi. "As a writer and editor, he was the very best that our generation will see."

Mr. Morris drank too much bourbon and red wine, smoked too many Viceroys, stayed up too late, and caroused too much. Indeed, friends have marveled at his ability to defy most of the conventions of good health. But, like his writing, his lifestyle betrayed a singular personality, given to long, rambling, evocative conversation, and the indelible stamp of growing up in another era.

He is survived by his wife, JoAnne Prichard of Jackson, and his son, David Rae Morris of New Orleans.

RICK BRAGG

The mourners said the same thing over and over: Willie Morris should have been here, to tell about this.

Mr. Morris, one of the most beloved writers of the modern South lay in state in the rotunda of the Old Capitol today as hundreds of people circled round and round, gazing at the closed dark-wood coffin, covered in white flowers, before moving on to hug his wife JoAnne Prichard, her tired face drifting somewhere between a smile and a sob.

"Willie would have loved this," she said.

"Oh," said his thirty-nine-year-old son, David Rae Morris, "he does."

A man who believed in ghosts, especially the Mississippi kind, would certainly come back to hear what was being said about him, old friends mused, many of them renowned writers who came to pay their last respects and to tell one last story of hard drinking in Manhattan, graveyard walks in Mississippi, and the lovely words he wrote about it all. That is why so many people here smiled, and even laughed out loud, in his still presence.

His ghost, they said, or his spirit, or—this being Mississippi, where people talk about God without feeling funny about it—his soul, will fly free every time someone cracks open one of his books about home, about family, about cats and dogs, and about finding peace in all of it.

"Willie liked the graveyard," said one long-time friend, David Halberstam, who wrote about Vietnam for *Harper's* when Mr. Morris, in self-imposed exile from Mississippi, was the magazine's editor-in-chief, in the late 1960s and early '70s.

"He came from the South at a time when you had to leave the South in order to find your voice," Mr. Halberstam said. "This," he said, looking around at the dignified Old Capitol and the line of people moving through the door, "may be the train that brings him home."

It has been years since state government occupied the Old Capitol, which is now essentially a museum. By unanimous decision of the board of the state's Department of Archives and History, which runs the place, Mr. Morris, who died in Jackson on Monday at the age of sixty-four, became the only writer ever to lie in state in its rotunda and only the third person in this century. (The others were former Senator John C. Stennis, who died in 1995 and former Governor J. P. Coleman in 1991.)

"The state of Mississippi knows how to treat a writer," said Pat Conroy, the best-selling author of *The Prince of Tides* and *The Great Santini*, among other books.

Mr. Morris was one of this state's best-known names, known for his *North Toward Home*—an anthem for countless writers who have turned toward New York as a validation of their craft, their worth—and for other works that painted a vivid picture of a man who badly wanted to love a flawed, angry place, and ultimately did. In 1967, he reached the heights of literary society by becoming, at the age of thirty-two, the youngest editor-in-chief *Harper's* ever had. He led the magazine through a golden era, hiring some of the best writers in the nation to examine civil rights, Vietnam, and the time's other issues. He was the talk of New York, and he loved it. When he resigned in 1971, at war with management, almost the entire staff quit with him.

But state officials say it was not anything he accomplished in New York that earned him the place here in this rotunda, on a day hot but, as if in deference to a native son, not particularly sticky. Rather, it was what he accomplished here, for Mississippi.

"He saw us overcome by all that bitterness, bigotry, and rage," said William Winter, who was governor in the early 1980s and later Mr. Morris's neighbor on a quiet Jackson street. From the 1960s on, Mr. Morris wrote "about civility, kindness, and tolerance, as an antidote," the former governor said.

Among the people who came to bid farewell today were literary types he had helped somehow along the way and perfect strangers who had read his words and just wanted to say good-bye. One of them, a house painter from Tuscaloosa, Alabama, just shook his head when asked why he had come, and said, "How could I not?"

Mr. Halberstam came to see an old friend. "I think of his sweetness," he said, "of the little boy who lived too long and too well." He remembers a Chinese restaurant with terrible food where Mr. Morris insisted on eating in the New York days. Mr. Morris, he said with a smile, liked the bar. The food did not much matter.

After the event in the rotunda today, Mr. Morris's coffin was driven about thirty-five miles north to his hometown, Yazoo City, the setting for many of his stories. Among a crowd of some 800 people that filled the First United Methodist Church there for a funeral service was Harriet DeCell Kuykendall, who told the mourners that Willie had always been a great storyteller, though not particularly good at math.

"I taught Willie algebra," she said. "He said he liked me better than algebra. And I knew that to be the gospel truth."

Then she read a passage from *North Toward Home*, in which Mr. Morris talked about how much dignity there was in dying in a small town, as against dying in a big one, and about the Yazoo City graveyard where he liked to walk.

"The cemetery itself held no horror for me," he wrote. "It was set in a beautiful wooded hill overlooking the whole town. I loved to walk among the graves and look at the dates and the words on the tombstones. I learned more about the town's past here, the migrations, the epidemics, the old forgotten tragedies, than I could ever have learned in the library. Sometimes we would bring our lunch."

This afternoon his friends laid Willie Morris to rest in that same cemetery. As a member of a marching band he had played taps for the American Legion whenever a soldier was buried there, and at the end of the graveside service today two buglers played taps for him.

PRESIDENT BILL CLINTON

It was early in 1968 when I met Willie Morris in New York. Morris was the editor of *Harper's* and had been a Rhodes Scholar. I wrote him shortly after I got my Rhodes, and to my surprise, he agreed to see me. He was wonderfully wry and funny—the classic southerner. He wrote a great book about his dog. He wrote a fascinating book about the role of football in the South and the racial barriers, *The Courting of Marcus Dupree*. You know, most southerners thought they'd be looked down upon if they went up to the Northeast. The cultural elites would all think they were hayseeds—although that was kind of phony; the *New York Times* was largely run by southerners—but there was always this sensitivity about how you'd be seen. Willie gave us another way of thinking about the South.

You know, for most of my generation of southerners who went north, the book that stuck in their minds was [Thomas Wolfe's] *You Can't Go Home Again*. Willie's *North Toward Home* was a beautifully written, evocative portrait of one person's love for the South who had profound regret over the racial situation. It helped a lot of people like me who wanted to see the world and do well up north but also come home and live in the South. He showed us how we could love a place and want to change it at the same time. It was really an important thing he did for me. He showed us we could go home.

RAAD CAWTHON

There is a passage early on in *North Toward Home* where Willie Morris, then twenty-two, finds himself in Paris and telephones the writer Richard Wright. Morris introduces himself as a "white . . . boy" from Yazoo City, the town on the edge of the Mississippi Delta that both Morris and Wright called home.

"We went to an Arab bar and got a little drunk together, and talked about the place we both had known," Morris wrote. "I asked him, 'Will you ever come back to America?' 'No,' he said. 'I want my children to grow up as human beings.' After a time a silence fell between us, like an immense pain—or maybe it was my imagining."

Even then Morris had the history of his people imprinted on his soul. In later years, Morris, who died this week at sixty-four, said, "Mississippi is America writ large," knowing just what that meant. It was his gift that in his best writing, *North Toward Home* or *The Courting of Marcus Dupree*, Morris was able to show us what that meant.

In 1981, when I first met Morris he was forty-six and had already returned from New York, the place he referred to as the "Kingdom of the Yankee," to live in a little faculty cottage on the campus of the University of Mississippi where he was writer-in-residence. All of us then, wishing to be the youngest Turks of southern journalism, knew of Morris. He was a Mississippian and a Rhodes Scholar, a former editor of *The Texas Observer*, and the youngest editor ever of *Harper's* magazine. In his 1967 memoir, *North Toward Home*, Morris gave voice to a generation fighting through the dense thicket of what it means to be a white southerner in America, possessed by a land whose more benighted history repels us, casting us out only to be called home again.

Like many before him, Morris had left the South in order to understand it. Wasn't it Quentin Compson's roommate at Harvard who asked in *Absalom, Absalom!* about that strange landscape of the South? What do they do there, he asked, how do they even live?

Morris did more than survive. He was brilliant, a blazing star of an editor who used *Harper's* magazine as a prism to refract the terrible struggles of his time. Morris turned over the pages of the magazine to David Halberstam writing about Vietnam and Larry L. King writing about Washington. A huge chunk of Norman Mailer's "The Steps of the Pentagon" filled an entire issue. Another issue carried a large section of *The Confessions of Nat Turner*, William Styron's novel and meditation on race in America.

That parsimonious owners had ultimately forced Morris out of his editorship only enhanced his luster.

By the time of Morris's return to Mississippi in 1980 a southerner had occupied the White House for four years. The South seemed suddenly ascendant. It became easy to believe that the best place from which our country could examine itself was from the bloody, haunted ground of the Old Confederacy. And it was Mississippi that was the bloodiest and most haunted of all places.

For anyone wanting to write about the nation's condition, Morris's return from self-imposed exile was an indication it was no longer necessary to leave our heart's terrain in order to truly be American, rather than solely southern, or to be taken seriously as a voice in the country's internal dialogue.

That night in Oxford, Morris became Willie. He stopped being an icon as we closed down the bar and left for his cottage with a case of Mexican beer riding shotgun in the backseat of his decrepit car. Having no cooler and worried about how to cool the hot beer, Willie had resolved the problem by casually tossing over the top of it the ice from a five-gallon bucket.

For the first time Willie demonstrated to me what I would see repeatedly through a friendship lasting the last seventeen years of his life. Generous of spirit, the most intelligent man I have ever known, one of Willie's joys was to share his knowledge.

I left Mississippi to Willie and moved on, finding my way eventually, as he had done, to the Yankee kingdom. But I saw him often, and in all those years Willie never failed to bolster my spirit and ego. He would tell me, "You're a writer, damn it!" Each time, by his generosity of spirit, Willie introduced me, however unworthy I felt, into a proud and closed fraternity.

As a friend said this week, "He gave so much of his heart away he didn't have any reserves left when he needed them."

Willie wrote fifteen other books after *North Toward Home*, and he never lost the genius of making the language perform for him. In his nonfiction novella, *The Fumble*, Willie remembers Katie, the long-ago girlfriend in Yazoo City who danced close "with her fingers casually on the lobe of my ear."

"Leaves of a dozen colors drifted down out of the trees in those sad and wistful days, those sad, horny Delta days," he wrote. "We remember what we wish to remember; it is all there to be summoned, but we pick and choose—since we are what we are—as we must and will be . . . I gaze down the summit of a quarter of a century, living in the Kingdom of the Yankee, all the accumulated losses and guilts and shames and rages, the loves come and gone, and death, ravenous death, and I summon now that instant standing in the shade of the chestnut with Katie Culpepper, herself long dead, buried under a mimosa on the hill in our cemetery far away, and I am caught ever so briefly in a frieze of old time, skinny and tall and seventeen, and senior year stretching before me as a Lewis Carroll dream, beckoning: 'Come, lad.'

"Artifice, all of it. They were burying the Korean dead . . . "

As a boy in high school Willie played taps for those Korean War dead returned home to the same cemetery on the hillside in Yazoo City where he and Katie Culpepper both now lie.

Willie's funeral was at the Methodist Church in Yazoo City. It was held there because, though he once wrote, "One cannot move along at a crisp rate on a steady diet of salvation," Willie was baptized a Methodist and the high school's gym, the locale favored by the family, is not air-conditioned. Two of Willie's favorite hymns, "Abide with Me" and "Amazing Grace," were sung. "Darkness on the Delta," a spiritual-blues penned by another lost Delta soul, was played. The service ended with taps.

Not played was "As Time Goes By," a favorite of Willie's. The fundamental things do apply as time goes by.

Will Campbell, who Willie once referred to as "the pastor to everyone in the Deep South," led the service along with William Winter, the former Mississippi governor whose progressive tenure corresponded with Willie's return from New York and whose Jackson neighbor Willie eventually became. Mike Espy, the Yazoo City native and former agriculture secretary who was the first black elected from Mississippi to the U.S. House of Representatives since Reconstruction spoke, as did Willie's high school algebra teacher.

In his eulogy, Styron, author of *Sophie's Choice*, referred to Willie's "elegantly furnished mind."

Willie, who was sentimental, who loved cemeteries and dogs, bourbon and red wine, conversation and children, Southeastern Conference football and the music he called, "the old songs," would have loved it all. He would also have loved the less formal moments, the returning of his scattered

Mississippi tribe for the occasion and the loud and liquid wake.

Willie loved the nights. During his *Harper's* years Willie held court at Elaine's, a Manhattan watering hole. Years later, at places like Hal and Mal's in Jackson, Lusko's in Greenwood, or Doe's Eat Place in Greenville, he was at his best at the head of a long and crowded table.

One such table, on a night not long after I first met him, was at The Sizzler, a steak house on the outskirts of Oxford. I was a columnist for the *Clarion-Ledger*, the Jackson newspaper, and Willie had invited me to speak to his writing class.

After the class, we all adjourned to the restaurant where, following the meal, Willie asked for quiet and launched into a long, flowery speech concerning my wonderful writing ability. My work, he said, had helped change Mississippi for the better. Reaching below the lectern, Willie brought forth what he assured everyone was an award from the university, describing it as something just short of a Nobel Prize.

It was only when I got to the lectern, accompanied by the applause of the table, that I realized the award was one of the dusty, old bowling trophies Willie had temporarily pilfered from a shelf running high around the room.

The words he wrote are many and mostly good. The stories are many and mostly good as well.

I could write of the night we spent in Greenville drinking with the Arkansas governor who would one day be a two-term president of the United States. Or of the day Willie scared the bejesus out of the son of a friend at the old witch's grave in Yazoo's cemetery. Or sitting around a motel swimming pool in Greenville and talking about marriage, women, and love, until the sunrise glinted amber through the two fingers of George Dickel left in the bottle.

But, in the end, it is not about the stories or even, amazingly, about what he wrote. It is about what a good friend Willie was, not just to me, but to all of us, that community of humans, southern and non-southern alike, who struggle with the perilous nature of our humanity.

"When I see an honored friend after years of separation, it is like reassuming the words of an old conversation which had been halted momentarily by time," Willie once wrote. "Surely, as one gets older, friendship becomes more precious to us, for it affirms the contours of our existence. It is a reservoir of shared experience, of having lived through many things in our brief and mutual moment on earth."

Well said, Willie. Well said.

CHAD CLANTON

Willie Morris and I first became acquainted over cheese enchiladas at Matt's El Rancho in South Austin. The University of Texas had invited him back to his beloved alma mater to address the LBJ School of Public Affairs. Many years had passed since his last trip to Austin and since he had been in Longhorn country. He was overjoyed. Midway through our meal Willie paused for a moment, taking in the scene, leaned in and whispered, "This is *magic!*"

But everything Willie did was magic. Because he made it magic. I'm not talking about something supernatural, although sometimes it seemed that way. Willie's magic was his unique ability to speak to the best parts of ourselves, both in his books and in person, and to make them better.

When he passed away last week in Jackson, Mississippi, he left behind perhaps the most vivid personal chronicles of a southerner's arguments with and allegiances to his Mississippi home. What made Willie's life and work so compelling, I believe, was his emotional honesty and youthful sense of humor. He took writing seriously, but he didn't always take himself seriously. In fact, he was a notorious prankster.

His pranks even extended to the Oval Office. Last fall during the impeachment drama, Willie and I were eating lunch at the White House with our dear mutual friend, Paul Begala, the brilliant Clinton strategist from Sugar Land. Just before dessert arrived, Begala's beeper sounded. "Sorry, boys, we gotta go . . .," he abruptly said. Neither Willie nor I dreamed the suffix to that sentence would be "to see the president."

President Clinton was a senior at Georgetown University when he discovered *North Toward Home*, Willie's mythic memoir. It moved him so profoundly that he traveled to New York to meet the author, who at that time was editor of *Harper's* magazine. Though the visit was brief, Willie always remembered it fondly. They became reacquainted in the 1980s and have been friends ever since.

What was likely intended to be a short photo-op turned into nearly half an hour of wonderful storytelling—an art both Clinton and Morris mastered in their native South. During one of Willie's tales, the president brought out a tin of gourmet cookies that Palestinian leader Yasser Arafat had recently given him—scrumptious cookies befitting the leader of the free world. We each took several. Little did I know Willie was working his magic, again.

Leaving the White House in a cab, we shared our separate observations from our presidential encounter. I told Willie that Arafat's were the best cookies I'd ever eaten. "I completely agree," he said with a mischievous grin, obviously concealing something more. Pulling three of the famous cookies from his coat pocket as if he were producing a rabbit from a hat, he said, "Chad, here, would you like another?"

In addition to his sunny humor, Willie was known for his constant, if not overgenerous, encouragement to young writers. He knew the greatest gift he could give them was confidence. Once, I sent him an essay, seeking his editing expertise and advice. A few days later, it appeared in my mailbox with excellent suggestions and a hand-written note, "You're a damn fine writer," it read. "Keep the faith, my friend!" That letter now hangs above my desk at home and continues to inspire.

To paraphrase Twain, the great people in life are the ones who tell others that they can be great, too. If that is true then Willie Morris was undeniably one of the great people.

Thursday at his funeral in Yazoo City, I remember the

lessons my friend and mentor Willie Morris taught me and countless others: Treasure people. Always trust your instincts. Fight for your beliefs. Marry a good woman. And when you get the chance, try to make some magic.

RICK CLEVELAND

His next book was going to be about baseball. Willie Morris, who loved baseball almost as much as he loved words, would have written a grand slam.

He already had his title, his first paragraph and his last. His wife, JoAnne Prichard, the remarkable lady whose love and inspiration surely added ten precious years to Willie's life, showed me his office the other day. There, on his table, were scads of index cards, clippings and notes written on cocktail napkins. They were arranged in rows, up and down the table, Willie's unique manner of outlining a book.

"One for My Daddy: A Baseball Memory" was the title. It would have been a personal memoir, the kind that brought out the best in Willie. It would have been about a father and his son and the son's son. It would have been about baseball within the broader contexts of their lives. It would have been about how baseball links fathers and sons and creates continuity through the generations.

It would have been a joy.

"He couldn't wait to write it," JoAnne said. "I've never seen Willie so excited about a book. This was one he had been thinking about for a long time. He was itching to get at it."

All writers, regardless of ability, learn through experience that we write best about what we care about most. That's why Willie wrote so brilliantly, so insightfully about Mississippi— "too small to be a country, too big to be an insane asylum"— and its people. That's why some of his sports stories, among them *The Fumble* and *Always Stand in Against the Curve,* are among the best in our language.

That's why his baseball book would have been a classic. Warner Alford, then the athletic director at Ole Miss, introduced me to Willie about this time of the year eighteen years ago in Oxford. Willie was the writer-in-residence there, having returned home from Yankeeland. At the time, I was covering Ole Miss for this newspaper [*Clarion-Ledger*]. We became fast friends immediately, sharing a love of sports, of the emotions they evoke, and mostly of the people who play them. I was, and still am, in awe both of what author William Styron would call Willie's "elegantly furnished mind" and his gentle soul.

"You know, Ricky," Willie once told me, "I am and always will be a sports writer at heart."

I loved Willie like a brother, like a trusted friend, like a favorite coach, and sometimes like a father after my own passed away. And he loved me. This I know because part of the sweetness of Willie was that he never failed to tell me so. He loved my children, as well. And they loved him, alternately like a godfather and like another playground playmate. Even at sixty-four, Willie had the spirit of a ten-year-old. I count it among the greatest of blessings that my children knew him and knew him well.

We often shared stories about our fathers and how they got us started writing. Willie was twelve when he began writing sports for the *Yazoo Herald.* I was thirteen when I began covering games for *The Hattiesburg American.* Both our fathers bought us our first typewriters, his a Smith-Corona, mine an Underwood.

Willie loved to tell about how he left the score out of his first game story. And he also loved to tell about when he sometimes played in the games he wrote about. He starred as a center fielder for an American Legion state championship team.

He led Yazoo High in hitting in baseball and free-throw shooting in basketball his senior year. "Hardwood" Kelly, his high school coach, was at Willie's funeral and reminisced about those days.

"Willie was a really good basketball player, but he was a natural in baseball," Kelly said.

Later, Willie became a really good fan. He loved his Ole Miss Rebels and became close with many of the coaches and athletes. He loved Jake Gibbs and Dog Brewer. He loved Alford and Ed Murphy and Rob Evans and Rod Barnes.

Ed Murphy, the ex-Rebel basketball coach, drove over from Georgia for the funeral. He talked about how Willie used to go on road trips with Murphy's teams, at times even sit on the bench. Willie always wanted to talk basketball; Murphy always wanted to talk about books. Willie also became close friends with Ed's son, Sean Murphy, now an intensive care doctor in North Carolina.

Said Ed Murphy, "Sean is around death every day of his life now, but when I told him about Willie's death he cried like a baby."

So many stories to tell, and not nearly enough space to tell them:

• About the time Willie and my wife were the last two fans sitting through a brutal rain and hail storm in the south end zone stands at Vaught-Hemingway Stadium. It was late in the fourth quarter and Johnny Majors's Tennessee Vols were putting an equally brutal whipping on the Rebels. I asked Willie and Liz what in the heck they were doing, huddled cold and soaked with lightning striking all around. Replied Willie, with no hesitation, "Waiting for snow." (Later, Liz told me that during the third quarter Willie reached into his pocket, pulled out a soaking wet fifty-dollar bill and hollered to all around, "Fifty dollars for anything dry!" There were no takers.)

• About the time Johnny Majors showed up for Willie's sixtieth birthday party. He had been a reader of Willie's and had written him fan letters, but the two had never met. JoAnne sent Majors an invitation, and Majors flew down from Pittsburgh, a most pleasant surprise. He and Willie drank whiskey, played piano, and sang songs well into the next morning. (No, there is no recording, and, trust me on this, that's for the best.)

• About Willie's sheer, boyish glee following trips to Lorman to watch Steve "Air" McNair. "Ricky," Willie gushed. "He's even better than you said he was. You must write a book about him!"

• About the time last summer when Majors and Willie and I and some other friends watched Mark McGwire hit his 62nd home run in Willie's den. Majors jumped off the couch cheering. Willie soaked it all in, smiling broadly and with a tear rolling down his cheek. "Look," he said, pointing at the portrait of Babe Ruth on his wall, "I think the Babe just cracked a smile."

• About our last trip together, to Starkville for Cool Papa Bell Day. That surely would have been part of Willie's book, because it was such a memorable day. After the ceremony, during which Willie gave a warm, thoughtful speech, he and I drove out to the ramshackle house where Cool Papa was born and raised. And we sat there and talked about what it is about Mississippi that makes so many smalltown boys, black and white—from places like Starkville, Columbia, Kiln, Drew, and Yazoo City—into national heroes. "I think," Willie said, "it's about the land and our closeness to it."

• About the times Willie scared the bejesus out of my kids at the witch's grave in Yazoo, where he now lies exactly thirteen paces away from the witch herself. He would love that.

• About Willie's joy when he found out that my son would be the pitcher who strikes out little Willie Morris in the soon-to-be-released movie *My Dog Skip*. Of Willie showing Tyler movies like *Rudy* and *Bang the Drum Slowly* and making sure my boy understood the messages therein. Willie knew those sports movies and others, like *Hoosiers*, by heart.

• About the night when Willie learned of my daddy's death. In New Orleans on a book tour, he walked out onto the French Quarter street, hailed a cab, told the cab driver that a good friend's daddy had died and that he needed a ride. To Jackson. The ride cost three hundred dollars, and by the time they reached Willie's house, he and the driver were buddies.

• About so many nights, so many toasts, so many stories, so many practical jokes, so much fun, so much advice and encouragement, so much loyalty, and so fine a friend.

The first paragraph of Willie's book would have begun with a description of the earliest memory of his life, when his father took him to a place called Goose Egg Park to introduce him to baseball using cardboard squares for bases, a small wooden bat, and a rubber ball. Willie was three.

"Every time I drive by there nowadays, I remember this," Willie wrote. "I recall the precise spot where Daddy laid out the minuscule diamond, the way he stood before me with the little wooden bat. 'Always swing level—see? Not up and down—LEVEL! Always look right at the pitcher. Look at his eyes.' His words ring out at me now across the concourse of the years."

Willie planned to end the book with a scene from a softball game played years and years later on Long Island. Willie played for a team of writers and politicians against a team of actors and musicians. His team was behind by two runs, and there were two runners on with two outs in the last inning. Dustin Hoffman was on the mound, Willie at the plate. Willie, suffused with deep thoughts of his father, swung and connected.

"The ball soared well over the tennis court wall in left center field and, as I crossed second and looked back, was bouncing mightily into the Hamptons, Long Island, distance. The last I saw of it, it was rolling toward Highway 25, the most wealthy, aristocratic, celebrity highway of all America."

As he crossed home plate, Willie stepped in a small hole and broke his ankle.

The book would have closed in the emergency room of a hospital with the doctor asking Willie: "Was it worth it?"

"Yes, Doctor," Willie wrote. "It was."

We can only imagine—and ache for—what would have connected Goose Egg Park to Long Island. Surely, it would have made us think, made us laugh, and made us cry, the way Willie always did.

We will miss his words, his essays, his stories, his ineffable way with the language. But those of us who knew him well will miss Willie all the more.

PAUL GREENBERG

It always hits you as a surprise, a stunner, a sudden shadow when you're busy with something unimportant. Walking into a hamburger joint in Pine Bluff for a quick lunch, a friend opens the screen door for you and mentions that Walker Percy just died. Or you're weeding out your e-mail in Little Rock when another friend copies an AP obit to you: "Mississippi author Willie Morris dies after heart attack . . . "

Oh no. After the shock, the anger, the irritation at it all sets in: What's this about *Mississippi* author? Of course Willie Morris was a Mississippi author, the way Walker Percy was a Louisiana author or Flannery O'Connor a southern author or Mark Twain or William Faulkner an American author . . . but you get the point. There are some writers, poets, people who are so rooted in their native soil, who are such *types*, that they belong to the world. The more local, the more universal. Like a vintage wine that is cherished at home, known abroad.

Great writers need not go wide to go deep. Usually it's the other way 'round. Faulkner's Yoknapatawpha County is a world, while the Internet is only a virtual world. Sherwood Anderson's *Winesburg, Ohio*, Thornton Wilder's *Our Town* . . . they're every place.

Willie Morris understood. He was so Mississippi that he was also necessarily, superbly southern and therefore inseparably and uncomfortably American. It's the fate southerners long have struggled with, but Willie Morris had the wisdom to embrace it, run with it, delight in it. He was such a typical southerner that he could hardly wait to leave, and years later hardly wait to get back.

At some point in his youth, Willie even managed to annex Texas to the South in the course of setting the world afire for the *Texas Observer*. Even now some of us still love the *Observer* for its golden youth, and that youth was largely a creation of Willie Morris, Ronnie Dugger, Larry L. King, Roger Shattuck, and assorted buddies who went on to become great authors— but may never again have had so much fun in their lives.

Willie Morris would go on to New York as the youngest editor of *Harper's* in its staid history, giving it a good dose of the language the way you might administer turpentine to a horse, right up the digestive tract. It's not easy. Above all, you need to remember to stand aside, and Willie Morris couldn't, not always. *Harper's* needed his shock treatment too much, sluggish thing it was pre-Morris.

You can't go around returning magazines to life without upsetting the kind of editorial pallbearers who feel you're putting them out of dreary work. After a few years of magazine doctoring, Willie headed south toward home, to Mississippi, epicenter of the southern language, and to write, write, write . . . and live, live, live. Right where he belonged, restless as he was.

Dead at sixty-four, the obit said. Too young, too soon, is everyone's first reaction. But no matter at what age we had lost Willie Morris, it would have been too young, too soon. He was not just a mirror of the South but a mirror that talked back, one that was always about ready to jump out of the frame and run off. Not just a reflection but a bourbon-drinking, storytelling response and, when necessary, rebuke. Over the years he somehow became an elder without losing the spirit of his youth.

Naturally he was married to an editor. Every writer should be—to blue-pencil the text of a life, to assure the right amount of excess, to make the prose poetry, to keep life inside the margins but brim-full. Willie Morris chose the best of editors: JoAnne Prichard of the University Press of Mississippi.

If every book begins as a great idea and becomes a great chore, JoAnne is the kind of editor who keeps a book, like a life, the way it should be: fun, moving, on track, a great cooperative enterprise, building up steam and shooting off cinders like the Dixie Express. . . . At his death, there is consolation in this: in JoAnne he was blessed.

In honor of the tradition Willie Morris embodied, a final story: A homesick Southern newspaperman, stuck in a job up North and hating it, was handed a book one day by his boss, who couldn't see the point of it. The book was almost thrown his way, with a condescending snort, in the best Yankee fashion, the way you'd get rid of any discard. ("Here, it's about the South, I think. It sounds like the sort of thing you'd like.") The newspaperman didn't get anything done the rest of the day. From his Dilbert-like cubicle in the bowels of a big-city daily up North there came nothing but unseemly shrieks of laughter, deep sighs, an irrepressible tear or two, and at least one long rebel yell. A copyeditor looked in and asked if he was all right. All right? Hell, he was splendid. A little resolve that had been slowly forming like a limpid pool in the back of his mind had suddenly crystallized into realization and determination: He was leaving this place as soon as he could find a spot on any paper south of St. Louis. The book was *North Toward Home* by Willie Morris. On that day, at that time, in that place, it beat the tar out of W. J. Cash's *The Mind of the South* or anything else.

A lot of Southerners of a certain generation, the Walker Percy–Flannery O'Connor–Willie Morris generation, seem to have had a similar experience. To quote William R. Ferris, who as an academic studies southerners the way entomologists study insects, said this about Willie Morris and his book: "His work in *North Toward Home* became a mantra for southerners who fled the South seeking worlds where they could be free and open in their thought but could never escape the love–hate relationship all southerners carry within them about the place of birth."

North Toward Home remains a comfort, a cry, a hoot, a tribute to and exposé of the swirling southern mind, which is never more southern than in exile. Thank you forever, Willie.

ORLEY HOOD

He wore shorts and an old Polo shirt and sat on a folding chair. His dog, Pete, lay on the floor, his nose buried in a box of chicken bones. The Best Western motel in Oxford didn't rest on formality.

Our pack of haggard sports writers had just finished a banquet interview with Ole Miss football coach Steve Sloan. Every August, we'd fly to the SEC schools and talk to players and coaches. The universities bought our favor with slabs of prime rib and gallons of whiskey. And we'd write long useless stories about how the left guard had worked out all summer, and this was the year the home team was sure to make big noise.

"Orley, I'm Willie Morris," he said. "That's Pete, my dog. Look, why don't you grab that bottle of Jack Daniels over there on the bar and a bucket of ice. We have a lot to talk about." It didn't take long to conclude that Willie was good for the soul and bad for the body.

A few years later, he invited Raad Cawthon, Malcolm White, and me up to Ole Miss to speak to his creative writing students, who met at the Western Sizzler restaurant. Willie recalled later that Donna Tartt had been in that class. Our payoff was cheap wine and an old bowling trophy. At 3 a.m., we drove to the cemetery to pay respects to Willie's beloved black Lab, Pete, who was buried up the hill in the back. Then we went down to scrape mud off Faulkner's grave.

Pete, Willie said, had the better plot. But Pappy, he had the longer sentences.

He never grew up. That was part of his charm. Till the day

he died, which was Monday, Willie was still the kid who roamed the dusty streets of Yazoo City with his pals on sweaty summer afternoons. He loved to play elaborate jokes. He loved to ride the backroads on weekends, searching through the weeds for gravemarkers in dilapidated cemeteries.

He took me up to Satartia to see the gym at the old abandoned school. It was wooden, airless on a blistering day. *Hoosiers*, he said referring to the movie. They'll tear it down, he said, and then it will be gone. He could see Gene Hackman coaching from the bench. He could see the kid shooting the soft jump shot from the corner. He could see everything, including the two Dobermans in the stairwell. We backed out reverently.

Everybody he ran into, everything he touched, was a story. He loved telling tales. When he'd get to the best parts, he'd whisper. Everyone would lean in to hear. Willie loved small conspiracies.

When he moved back home to Mississippi he brought his pals with him. David Halberstam would come down. George Plimpton, too. William Styron, who loved Willie dearly, would come to dinner at the Governor's Mansion or give a lecture up at school. When Pete died, Styron was the first to call. "I was very worried about Willie," he said later.

I told Willie a few years ago that I wanted to do a story on famous people from Yazoo City. He said that would require the $10 tour. We rode around all afternoon, up in the hills and down in the flats. That's where Zig Ziglar lived. Haley Barbour. Willie Wood, the best football player ever. And Mike Espy. Willie grew up on Grand Avenue. "All my boyhood dogs are buried in that back yard," he said, "including Skip."

Willie leaned over as we drove through the gate of the cemetery where he used to blow taps for Korean War casualties. He whispered, "I know everybody here." When he's laid to rest on Thursday, there'll be no need for introductions.

RHETA GRIMSLEY JOHNSON

I avoided Willie Morris in Mississippi, which wasn't all that easy to do.

In Mississippi, you can say "Willie" the same way you say "Elvis," without using a surname, and people know who you mean. When Willie was writer-in-residence at Ole Miss, young reporters from Jackson kept the roads hot, making regular pilgrimages to Oxford. Everybody wanted to brag he'd met the famous editor-returned-home, to say they'd sat in a corner of the Holiday Inn and crooked an elbow with greatness. Word was, the sure way to get an audience with Willie was to visit his favorite watering holes.

If you were lucky enough to find him, Willie was most gracious, everyone agreed, and he never seemed to lord it over those of us who commit journalism on a daily basis. If you caught him on a really good night, the party might last into the wee hours and end up at Faulkner's grave, which was as good as it got.

Nobody admired his work more than I, especially his first and most famous book, *North Toward Home.* In that one, he describes tramping about New York, asking for work and being treated like a "pluperfect hick" by fancy, self-important editors. (In true Cinderella–Mississippi fashion, Willie soon became one of the most respected editors ever to worm his way into the Big Apple. And I think he really meant it when he wrote he'd never forget or copy that haughty treatment.)

Even so, I couldn't bring myself to join a parade of supplicants. I figured Willie had all the friends he needed.

But I finally did meet him. I interviewed Willie for this newspaper [*Atlanta Journal-Constitution*], and his charm lived up to his reputation. We had dinner at a restaurant where everybody knew him, and it wasn't so much a meal as a love feast. Willie's admirers kept stopping by the table to compliment him on one piece of writing or another, quoting whole passages by rote as if they were taking oral exams. Willie beamed, obviously enjoying the sound of his own words come alive. He kissed hands extended by pink and perfect Jackson belles and eventually spoke to everyone in the place, including the cook.

He told me he never read stories about himself, but I didn't believe it then and still don't. I think he'd just decided that great writers *shouldn't* read stories about themselves. But nobody ever got kinder press than Willie Morris. To write unkind things about Willie would have been to kick a puppy dog.

At one point in the evening, he grabbed my reporter's notebook and started a furious scribbling, as if he found it impossible to watch someone else writing while he was idle. It turned out to be a florid, loving description of Mississippi. I kept it for a long time, then discovered it was part of an essay he'd already had published.

Willie wrote a lot, and well, in his last few years, but it seemed to me he'd already told his best story, that first one. He became as much a goodwill ambassador for Mississippi as anything else, champion of the state everybody loves to hate. He was just more genial proof that, for whatever reason, Mississippi makes writers the way Michigan makes cars.

When I read he had died at sixty-four, I felt grateful to have met him. He'd been outlived by one of his literary heroes and neighbors, Eudora Welty, who turned ninety this year.

He once wrote he'd read Miss Welty's "A Worn Path" in the seventh grade, and it made him want to be a writer.

I think he knew there were those of us who were likewise inspired by him, by the way he made good, but never so good he forgot home.

DEBORAH MATHIS

It's one of life's sad facts that, as we age, our world begins emptying. One by one, people who have been there—always, it seems—slip the surly bonds. New people come in and although they enrich us in their own ways, we are somehow poorer for wonders we lost.

For example, there will never be another Willie Morris, the great writer and southern fellow whose heart stopped beating Monday night. Such a heart it was. Full of merriment and compassion and hospitality and, yes, mischief too.

Life was not always fair to Willie—is it to anyone?—but he relished it. The man loved a good time and could usually be counted on to provide it. Like the night I first met him, ferried to his and wife JoAnne's home by a friend who understood that no Mississippi sojourn would be complete without at least once meeting Willie.

There were candles on the dinner table that night and a huge bowl of spaghetti, a basket of bread, a large salad, and great red wine. For hours we talked about writing, about language, about vocabulary games we invented for ourselves, about Southernness, about politics, about religion.

At one point, Willie asked his wife and editor, JoAnne Prichard, to "go back there and get them what I've been working on." It was his next book, he explained, and he wanted us to hear chapter 1.

Shortly, JoAnne returned with several white pages. "Chapter 1," she began. "I came to the city, and it changed my life."

I was immediately entranced. And envious. Such plain wording and, yet, they had me. It was the beginning of *New York Days*, one of Willie's last books.

When it was published, I took great pride in remembering how I had been there at the beginning. I was happy, too, that neither Willie nor his editor had tampered with the opening line, though it might have noted that, as the young editor of *Harper's* magazine, Willie changed the city's life, too.

By the end of the reading, Willie was ready to indulge his guests. "Let's get in the car and drive down to Yazoo City and see the witch," he said. Growing up in the small Delta town, he had often visited the gravesite of an allegedly supernatural woman.

"Let's get in the car and go now," he said. It was almost midnight. Yazoo City was two hours away. There was work tomorrow. There had already been too much wine. But Willie was dead serious. Fortunately, he was too gentle a spirit to insist.

Willie Morris was one of my heroes, one of my role models. I admired his cellular understanding of human nature, his deep sweet love of the crazy, double-edged South, his mastery of words, and his wisdom in putting them together.

I had counted on him to help me through my first book, whenever that might be. Unlike some writers who are stingy with their talent, Willie loved to share his. He liberally gave advice. "Follow the chronological order," he told me after going over one of my early attempts. "Just tell the story as it happened."

He also urged me to write my book "down here," meaning the South generally and, I believe, Mississippi particularly. Willie believed there was something about the Deep South that nourished the imagination and the ability to reduce it to colorful words. He probably had a point.

The South was home to an inordinately large fraternity of

great penmen and penwomen—Faulkner and Welty and Williams and Ford and Lee . . . and Morris. There is indeed, something about the place that fertilizes the mind.

There are new great writers in the wings who will inspire and educate and entertain. But Willie, with his brilliant mind and sterling heart, was one of a kind. I dare say that I came to know him, and it changed my life.

BILL MINOR

I am proud to have been in the legion of FOWs—friends of
Willie.

That's Willie Morris, of course. Our friendship went back
thirty years.

Some have said he was Mississippi's second William
Faulkner, with shorter sentences. However, Willie's characters
were real live folks, not fictional. Unless you include *The Last
of the Southern Girls,* the novel that obviously resembles his un-
fortunate first marriage.

Perhaps we all never realized how appropriate it was he
had the name Willie, signifying the countrified kid who never
grew up. Oxford on a Rhodes Scholarship didn't change that,
neither did fifteen years among the literati of New York City.

My first recollection of meeting Willie was finding him
torn between wanting to live both in New York and Mississippi, and with a wild notion of spending six months each
year in each place.

He was only in his early thirties then, a mere kid, editing
one of the nation's oldest magazines, *Harper's.*

Inevitably, Willie, the garrulous southerner, and the staid
Harper's ownership parted ways several years later. Then it was
only a question of time before he would come back to the
land that he loved. He was back to stay in 1980. Legend are
the stories people have related since his sudden death of how
Willie Morris touched their lives.

Mine has to do with his first book, *North Toward Home,*

which brought us together for a springtime evening of dining and imbibing in 1970, when our oldest son, Paul, was in the Army, serving in Vietnam. Willie vowed he would inscribe a copy and send it to Paul.

As we later learned, this was a particularly difficult period for Paul, and the arrival of *North Toward Home* lifted his spirits immeasurably, renewing his hope that he, too, would come home alive within a few months. When Paul did return from Vietnam, thankfully with sound body and mind, Willie's book came with him and is prized today.

In the early 1970s, Willie would bounce into town working on *Yazoo*, which touched on how his old hometown, Yazoo City, and Mississippi were dealing with massive desegregation of public schools and the rise of private academies.

Going to dinner (usually a warm-up beforehand), with Willie was always something I virtually feared, not because of the wonderful conversations, but the aftermath. When Willie had finished eating, he was ready for round two in his bout with the grape.

Two weeks before he died, my wife and I were having dinner at the Mayflower Cafe. Willie and JoAnne ambled in (the Mayflower was always his favorite) as we neared the end of our meal. Willie asked us to come join in a glass of wine when we had finished eating.

We did, and I vividly recall the plate of food put before Willie was not the broiled fresh fish for which the Mayflower is noted, but chicken fried steak smothered in flour gravy.

There's no one left I can think of with his literary credentials and a smidgen of his network of friends who can—and will—explain this baffling state and win compassion and understanding of it nationally.

It was so fitting that Willie, the quintessential good ole boy from Yazoo City, was the first Mississippi writer to lie in state in Mississippi's Old Capitol. Ineffable, Willie would say.

Sid Salter

Like many of the current generation of Mississippi journalists, Willie Morris taught me a lot about writing, about life, and about a writing life.

Interwoven in those lessons are the faces of fellow journalists, a beloved son, authors, educators, bartenders, restaurateurs, waitresses, coaches, athletes, the famous, the infamous, the nameless, and a dog named "Pete."

Willie was—by his own considered description—a "good ole boy."

I shall remember him that way. And while a mentor, a friend, and a guiding force in my own life and work, Willie remained from his childhood days in Yazoo City a gentle southern man particularly predisposed to kindness to the elderly, to children, and to animals—a good ole boy.

Despite his generosity of spirit, his easy, self-deprecating nature or his willingness to indulge the claims of strangers on his time, his energy, and his fame, Mississippi never produced a more ardent defender or a harsher social critic.

That conflict—Willie's love of home, family, and heritage tempered against his outrage at racism, hatred, and injustice—would color the whole of his life and his work.

I never presumed to have solved the riddle of Willie Morris during a twenty-year friendship, but I think redemption had something to do with it.

I think he believed in the basic goodness of the people of the South in general and Mississippi in particular—black and white and red—and was convinced that given enough time, enough reflection, and enough illumination from our better angels, we would ultimately do the right thing.

For my money, he joined the late William Faulkner and the enduring Eudora Welty in a league of their own as Mississippi's greatest literary talents—and in a state that produced the likes of Richard Wright, Richard Ford, Ellen Douglas, Tennessee Williams, John Grisham, and a host of other daunting literary figures, that's not idle praise.

I remember the company he kept during the early 1980s when I knew him well in Oxford while he labored over *The Courting of Marcus Dupree.*

On any given night, one could open the back door of his Faculty Row bungalow and find characters as diverse as William Styron, Larry McMurtry, David Halberstam, Winston Groom, George Plimpton, David Sansing, Gale Denley, Ed Perry, Charles Henry, Glenn Griffing, Ron Shapiro, Orley Hood, Rick Cleveland, Raad Cawthon, Mickey Spagnola, Lee "Scoop" Ragland, Dan Turner, Billy Watkins, and a revolving collection of students, barflies, and camp followers.

Like a literary Johnny Appleseed, Willie spread the gospel of the worth of writing to all who would listen. He encouraged young journalists by being overly generous with praise and instilled in us a sense of confidence most of us sorely needed. To miss that point and to overlook the access Willie gave a group of young Mississippi newspaper journalists to nationally-prominent writers—who were in most cases more in awe of Willie's writing talents than we were—is to miss why he was so much more than a writer.

Like the rest of us, Willie wasn't perfect.

The truth is Willie drank too much, smoked too much, slept too little, and indulged most every whim he ever entertained.

But he was responsible in a higher sense to his craft, to his public, and to portraying Mississippi in a realistic light in the eyes of the nation.

Willie Morris was not an apologist for Mississippi nor a partisan—he was a son of Mississippi burdened and bewildered by her past, observant and annoyed at times of her present, and hopeful for her future.

Late in life, after some tempestuous relationships, Willie found the love of a good woman. JoAnne Prichard's entry into Willie's life seemed to signal the end of his wanderings.

And over a glorious life that we in Mississippi have yet to fully recognize and honor, Willie Morris became wealthy— wealthy in friends, wealthy in the respect and affections of those he considered his peers, and wealthy in sharing with the world a talent to write given straight from God.

He was the best writer I've ever known. In writing of Yazoo City, Willie penned these lines: "The town where I grew up sits there on the edge of the Delta, straddling that memorable divide where the hills end and the flatland begins. The town itself was half hills and half Delta, only 40 miles from the Mississippi as the crow flies. . . . When the Greyhound out of Jackson stops at some dilapidated grocery store covered with patent medicine posters to pick up a few Negroes, or a solitary traveler waving a white handkerchief in the middle of nowhere, the driver will ask 'Where to?' and the passenger will say 'Yazoo,' with the accent on the last syllable, rich and bass like a quick rumble of thunder."

In Willie's Heaven, there will be Pete, Skip, and Mamie— and Ray and Marian. Ole Miss and LSU will play football in the mornings and State and Alabama will play baseball in the afternoons. At night, there'll be some etoufee at the Hoka with a bottle of Bolla and some chicory coffee.

And what stories he will tell—stories that God will want to hear.

MICHAEL SKUBE

In the end, there was a certain justice after all.

New York was the town Willie Morris both loved and hated, the city where he had made a name as a young man and the city that quickly forgot him once he was shown the door at *Harper's* magazine. Morris, who died Monday after suffering a heart attack at his home in Jackson, Mississippi, spent the better part of his adult life writing evocatively about the South and his native Mississippi. But for long years there was a shadow in his life, and it was the city he called Big Cave in his memoir *North Toward Home*, the story of a sports-loving, prank-playing boy who grows up in Yazoo City, Mississippi, wins a Rhodes scholarship at the University of Texas, and becomes one of the most talked-about young journalists of his generation.

Morris was sixty-four when he died and had been back to New York infrequently. The parade moved on, and Morris was living quietly if bibulously in Mississippi, first in Oxford, where he wasn't happy, and later in Jackson, where he was.

And then, last week, he and his wife, JoAnne Prichard, were in New York for a private screening of a movie based on his book *My Dog Skip*.

"He called me from up there, and he was excited," novelist Winston Groom, a friend since the 1970s, said from his home in Alabama. "He and JoAnne enjoyed themselves, and he said the Time Warner people liked the movie and had big plans for it. You can usually tell when they're blowin' smoke, but Willie was really looking forward to its coming out."

He was so excited he called another old writer friend, Larry L. King, from New York. "I think Willie felt great at the end," King says. "I think he went out on top."

People who knew him over the years had seen him at the bottom, in the years after he resigned as editor of *Harper's* in 1971—a resignation that the Cowles publishing family of Minneapolis, Minnesota, may or may not have forced but readily accepted.

"It devastated him," novelist and longtime friend William Styron said yesterday. "To be riding so high and then to be brought so low, it had to. I know Willie contributed to some of his problems, but I think it must have been comparatively minor. I don't know why the people out in Minnesota couldn't have had the imagination to realize he was putting out a first-class magazine. I'll never forget the avalanche of support he got from all over the world, thousands and thousands of letters."

He was only thirty-two in 1967 when he was editor-in-chief of *Harper's*, the youngest in its long and distinguished history. But when Morris took over, it was a magazine that was respected more than it was read. Morris quickly resuscitated it. He brought in David Halberstam to write about Vietnam, Betty Friedan to write about the sexes, Larry L. King to write about Washington, William Styron to write a 45,000-word piece about a slave rebellion that would become his Pulitzer Prize-winning book *The Confessions of Nat Turner*.

In 1968, at the height of Vietnam War protests, Norman Mailer's article "The Steps of the Pentagon" filled the entire magazine.

Morris appreciated good writing and was willing to pay for it.

For one brief, shining moment *Harper's* and Willie Morris were the talk of the town—and then the money men summoned him to a meeting in Minneapolis. When he resigned, the entire staff save one—current editor Lewis Lapham—left with him.

"Willie wasn't a bean counter, he was a writer's editor," Winston Groom says. "He was arguably the best line editor there ever was. He just had a reverence for writing. And he was so good with younger writers. If it hadn't been for Willie, I doubt I'd have ever left the *Washington Star*."

After leaving *Harper's*, Willie found sanctuary in an informal colony of writers who lived and drank on Long Island— George Plimpton, James Jones, Kurt Vonnegut, John Knowles, Irwin Shaw, Truman Capote, among them. "Truman's gone, Irwin's gone, Jim's gone," Groom says. "Willie was the glue that held us together."

Plimpton recalls Morris's trying to explain the South to him. "He took me to a football game one time," Plimpton says. "It wasn't Ole Miss, it was to see this fellow [Steve] "Air" McNair, who was quarterback for Alcorn State," Plimpton says. "I think we must have been the only two white people there.

"His great-great-grandfather impeached my great-great-grandfather, you know. Adelbert Ames was a Reconstruction governer of Mississippi, a Republican, and Willie's great-great-grandfather was on the committee that impeached him. So we'd stand there in the statehouse, and I'd salute my great-great-grandfather and he'd salute his."

In the years after he left *Harper's*, Morris wrote several books and sometimes needed cash between book advances. Groom remembers his stint as writer-in-residence at the now-defunct *Washington Star*. The paper had asked Groom, a court reporter who would one day become rich from his novel *Forrest Gump*, to show Morris around and look after him. "He was a mess, but he wrote some wonderful stuff for us," Groom says. "He could look at a telephone book and find a story in it.

"What happened at *Harper's* hurt him. Everybody knew that," Groom says. Not only did he lose his job, but his marriage collapsed during his years at *Harper's*, and his personal life went into a downward spiral that worried friends for years. He began drinking in the mornings. He was the subject of jokes, even among friends, and of a cruel profile in *The Washington Post.* His relationship with his teenage son, David Rae Morris, deteriorated.

At Willie and JoAnne Morris's home in Jackson on Tuesday, though, David Rae Morris, now thirty-nine and a photographer, said he and his father had reconciled. "We had our problems, like a lot of people," the younger Morris said, "but we talked a lot in the past few years. At the end, there was nothing left unsaid."

"Willie was a complex person with deep-seated problems," Styron recalls. "He needed to have a crutch of alcohol, and heavy doses of it. We both had the same love–hate relationship toward New York, and, like many writers, he had a propensity toward melancholy."

And then he met JoAnne Prichard, an editor at the University Press of Mississippi. "Willie told me JoAnne saved his life," Larry L. King says. They married and moved to Jackson in 1990, and there were spells when he drank less. But he was never out of its grip.

"Willie was not only a marvelous editor but a marvelous writer," Styron says. "And it's been well documented that writers are susceptible to alcoholism."

Friends who had seen him unhappy during the '70s and early '80s say it was Prichard who brought him what happiness he knew. And the happiness they say, was genuine.

In his book *New York Days* Morris wrote of the time and the experience that all but broke him. "I had not made the slightest ripple on this place, for New York somehow obliterates you, and especially the outlander." He understood, a few years shy of sixty, that the holy grail he sought as a young man was not the one he needed. "What I was looking for all the time was me, and I was not there."

He found it only when he turned south toward home.

DONNA TARTT

Thinking about Willie in these days since his death, this honorific comes again and again to mind: "the greatest of the Boys." It was said, originally, of Stephen Crane but it could be as easily said of Willie. Often I had the hilarious incredulous sense, being with Willie, of being with Huckleberry Finn all grown up—for who knew, really, what happened to Huck after he lighted out for the Indian territories? One can easily imagine Huck grown up (and out) into a big old tender-hearted man much like Willie: a practical jokester, a foe of injustice, a friend to all dogs; a man who loved taverns and old cemeteries, who poured big old slugs of bourbon into his coffee to warm himself up on chilly autumn nights. Like Huck, too, his happy carelessness for material comforts bordered on the vagabond—his raggedy sweaters, his torn tennis shoes, his modest little bachelor home back in the Oxford days before he married JoAnne, a house that was (except for an unframed photograph of his terrier, Skip, then twenty years dead) wholly unadorned. When we met, I was seventeen and he was in his late forties, but what I think struck me most about him was this great open-hearted quality of boyishness that he had, for he was far more boyish than most of the actual boys I knew at Ole Miss, passionless frat boys whose hearts had already narrowed and tightened (even at seventeen, eighteen, nineteen) into the hearts of the burghers and businessmen they would someday become.

Willie, on the other hand, was a boy in all the very best ways: quick to make friends, quick to take sides, quick to laughter and outrage and tears and mischief. Because of his unsuspicious good nature, he was not always so quick to defend himself, or to look out for his own best interests, but no one leapt more rapidly to the aid of a friend, and he mourned the disappointments of others as if they were his own. He had the boy's romantic way of thinking always about death, even in the raucous wholehearted tumble of life. Moreover, he had the boy's heroic refusal to accept some of life's more petty brutalities. The bonds of affection were not lessened for him—as they are for most people—by the fact of physical death. For him, the wounds were always fresh. In the midst of life, he continued to grieve for, and honor, his dead—everyone, all the little ones, down to the very dogs, in a way that calls to mind the Bodhisattva's vow: "However numberless sentient beings are, I vow to save them." If it were up to Willie, he would have saved them all, kept the doors of Heaven open until all Creation was safe inside: every hobo, every stray, every last june bug. (One of the lines he loved most, from *King Lear*: "The little dogs and all,/Tray, Blanch, and Sweetheart, see, they bark at me." To me, he said: "See now, darling, this is what makes Shakespeare a great poet. He remembers the little dogs, he calls them by their names." Then, glancing down at Pete the Labrador retriever, his constant companion of those days: "Shakespeare would have loved old Pete here, *wouldn't* he though? If old Pete was there, Shakespeare would have called Pete's name too, don't you think?")

Back when I was introduced to Willie, when I was just a kid myself, he was a great, mythical Mr. Micawber of a figure, walking the streets of Oxford in the late afternoons with his toes pointed out and his Ray-Ban sunglasses on. He grabbed me by the hand and pulled me down the street, so that I had to run to keep up with him, and it was as if we had known each other always. He was like that, I think, with all his friends: he knew them when he saw them, fell in step right alongside them, and loved them forever. "Would you like a Coca-Cola, young lady?" he asked me on that first night, interrupting himself in the middle of a story, when his old pal Clyde the bartender came around to take our order at the bar of the Holiday Inn.

"No, sir, I believe I'll have what you're drinking."

Terrific roar of laughter. "Why," he shouted, staggering back as if dazed by my prodigy, rolling his rich old eye round at the assembled company, "this girl is a WRITER!" When the bourbons arrived, he insisted that we clink glasses: "A toast."

"To what?"

"To you! To us! This is a *historic night!* Someday you'll be famous, you'll write about this very meeting, you'll remember it forever. . . . "

I was a little overwhelmed, with this big, drunk, famous person towering over me at the bar, proclaiming blood brothership, offering eternal friendship, thundering outlandish prophecies. But—God bless you, Willie!—you were right, because here I sit at the typewriter nearly twenty years later, recalling all this.

I lived right down the street from Willie that year, when I was seventeen and then eighteen, and I was lucky to get the chance then to know him so well and spend as much time with him as I did. We loved and hated a lot of the same things. Never will I forget my naive astonishment at discovering that there existed another person who loved words in much the same sputtering and agonized way that I did, who fought them and cursed them and cried over them and stood back dazzled and agog in admiration of them. After all those years isolated in my hometown, shut up in my bedroom reading books, I had thought I was the only person in the world so afflicted.

"Oh, no, honey. There's a lot of us out there. You'll meet them."

And I did. But he was the first, and the one I loved the best, and—when I look back through the years, at all the things I ended up doing that I never dreamed were possible, if I look back far enough I always see Willie, with his shirt untucked, standing at the very back of the room and blowing me a kiss.

Willie had his light moments, no doubt about it; he was a great phone prankster, chatting away straight-faced and unconcerned to one of his unsuspecting colleagues in the character of "Mae Helen Biggs" or "Clinton Roy Peel" or some such: "Yas suh!" he would cry. "I sho did see it! Yo car rolling down the street just now and an ole black dog sitting right up at the wheel. . . . " Afterward, he would hang up quite soberly—as if he'd just phoned to check on his bank balance—and not until some moments later (returning from the kitchen, fresh drink in hand) would he convulse with laughter, stricken all at once by the genius of the joke that he'd so brilliantly pulled off.

Rich companion that he was, Willie also suffered terribly. It was a commonplace among those who knew him—those who didn't love him, but also some who did—to attribute Willie's operatic range of emotion to drink. The truth was more complicated and had to do with that raw, gigantic, intensely tender heart of his about which we've heard so much in the last weeks, that heart which he seldom guarded or protected in any way but left right on the surface for the world to scratch at. What drink could palliate those ancient, chilling sorrows that settled over him? "How are your spirits, darling?" That is the first question, or among the first, he always asked—for, when he wanted to bend forward and look close, he could see into other people's hearts with a rather terrifying clarity. The word *spirit* was chosen quite carefully: for when Willie asked this question he was inquiring about your spirit in the sense of your mood, but also the state of your immortal spirit, your soul; about your spirits in the old, high-colored French sense (wit, sparkle, intelligence), and the spirits in your glass (did you need a refill?), and even your spirits in the sense of your ghosts, as in memories and people of the past (the recent past, a hundred or two hundred years past) which might be haunting you. All these things he was checking upon when he bent his head low and tried to catch your eye, like a waggish doctor, and asked his perennial question.

Further: he really wanted to know. And he wanted to do something about it. "Let's go get a steak. Let's drive over to Rowan Oak. Let's call up old George Plimpton in New York and talk to him on the telephone." If Willie thought you were sad, he'd stand on his head if he thought it might cheer you up. (I think of how I once saw him following his housekeeper around his Oxford home, in and out of rooms, ruthless as a bird dog, because he thought something was bothering her, and he had, absolutely had, to know what it was.) But in spite of his solicitude for others, Willie's own grief harrowed him continually; in many respects he was simply not at home here and by *here* I mean the world, with all its callousness and cruelties and forgetfulness; he was inconsolable, too haunted by the inferno of loss, by time, and change, and mutability. "Brightness falls from the air;/Queens have died, young and fair." Sometimes he would stop dead—in the middle of a sentence, in the middle of a room—as if sensing subterranean tremors. You could see it in his eyes then, that sickening awareness he had of the lurching, inescapable grind of time: time like sand, time sliding under our feet, time inescapable and relentless, time rolling forward—on all we love, and would like to save—with a sickle and a grin. And this too was a part of his genius. He was exquisitely calibrated to sense these dreadful underground rivers of sorrow, constantly quaking beneath the surface of everyday life; everybody senses them at one time or another, but Willie was so constituted that he was shaken by them constantly, and it is to this vertiginous but quite accurate awareness that he had, of time collapsing about us moment by moment and shifting beneath us, that I attribute his occasional unsteadiness on his feet—a sort of motion sickness of the soul. Though it's there all the time, this knowledge of the hourglass running out, time slipping away, most people don't feel it the way he did (at least not so constantly—else they couldn't get out of bed in the morning). But Willie—like a dog driven crazy by a whistle too high-pitched for the human ear—was constantly stricken by this inexorable motion that others, less sensitive, were unable to detect and because of it he could never quite recover his equilibrium, his balance. No wonder he liked to slosh a little bourbon in his coffee from time to time.

In some sense, Willie's preoccupations were those of the Chinese poets. Fallen blossoms, dewy stairs, and lost youth. The sorrow of leavetakings, farewell to friends, soldiers on the march, and geese flying south. His sense of history pained him, and so did his sense of beauty. I can easily imagine him—like the great Li Po—toppling drunken into the river while trying to embrace the moon. He was tremendously moved by things like fallen sports idols, aging movie stars, dead animals on the road. Forlorn or desecrated monuments in the cemetery. Rain and autumn bonfires. (Some neighbor hammering in a garage, on a foggy gray day in the winter: "Sounds like they're making somebody's coffin over there, darling.") When he was sad, sometimes he would ask me to recite poetry to him—poems I had learned in high school—which I didn't quite see the point of as they only seemed to make him sadder. Of my small repertoire, he especially liked Housman's "To an Athlete Dying Young"; "Annabel Lee"; and Gerard Manley Hopkins: "Margaret, are you grieving/Over Goldengrove unleaving?" It is the blight man was born for,
It is Margaret you mourn for.

He also liked to read aloud. Thomas Wolfe. The last page of *The Great Gatsby*. "So we beat on, boats against the current, borne back ceaselessly into the past." And he would lean back in his shabby chair and close his eyes with the relief of hearing someone else describe, so well, the rhythms that beat so ceaselessly against his own poor heart.

After I left Mississippi, at Willie's urging, to go to college in New England ("You've learned what you need to know here," he said to me, and he was right), we didn't see nearly so much of each other, though we certainly had our laughing glorious reunions in the years to come: after he'd married JoAnne and moved to Jackson, after I'd published my first book. (Perhaps my very happiest memory of Willie is a comparatively recent one of being in a hotel room in New Orleans, on tour for my first book, hearing a knock on the door and thinking it was housekeeping, but no, it was Willie, with JoAnne right behind him, Willie who grabbed me up and practically threw me in the air for joy. Still up to his old tricks: he'd deceived me with that timid little casual rap at the door, and neither of us could stop laughing about it. So many people were happy for me when I published my first novel, but apart from my mother, I don't think that anybody in the world was happier or more proud than he was.)

But it is much farther back—to that distant time when he and I were neighbors, and saw each other almost daily—to which my thoughts return again and again now that Willie has died. I've been thinking about his frequent visits to Faulkner's grave, and his scratchy old record of the song "Moon River"; he played it over and over when he was sad, and upon at least one occasion he played it so incessantly that I—and several other guests—were driven from his home. I think, too, how the movie *Casablanca* always made him cry—especially the scene where everyone stands up in Rick's Cafe and sings the "Marseillaise" in defiance of the Nazis. This episode was so important for Willie that it became a sort of shorthand, a code, a way for him to explain why he loved the people he did. "They'd sing the 'Marseillaise,'" he'd say, nodding across the room at someone he loved: Ron Shapiro, say, or Deanie Faulkner (how he loved Deanie!) or Masaru or David Sansing. "And Pete. Pete'd be right up there in the front, leading the band, wouldn't you, boy?"

Something else that comes to mind—I don't know why, but it does—is an evening I walked from my dormitory over to his chilly, little, bare house. That house, with its lawn never raked, deep in dead leaves, was sunk all the year round in a perpetual autumn. (There's a word, in French, for that particular still, sad quality that Willie's house had, in the early '80s, with the forlorn little picture of Skip the dead terrier propped up on the bare mantelpiece: *fadeur*. When I first came upon it, in Verlaine, I told Willie about it, and he got all excited, too. "Oh, that's a marvelous word. Nothing like it in English at all, is there? Pete, can you think of anything? Pete?")

I found Willie there, in the twilight, in his little *fadeur* house, sitting with his face in his hands without the lamp on, crying in the most desolate and brokenhearted way, so that I could not immediately understand what he was saying: "That girl," he cried, "that poor girl," and it was a while before I realized that he was crying for the movie star Natalie Wood, who (it was in all the papers that day) had fallen off a yacht and drowned.

I was stricken, sympathetic. Had she been a great friend of his?

"No," he cried, rolling his head back, "no, of course not, she was just so beautiful. . . . "

This recollection surfaced, from apparent void, two or three days after Willie's death, and it was so sharp and sudden that I flinched from it a little bit without quite knowing why: why had this odd fragment bobbed up so perfect and whole (I can still see the smoke spiraling from his cigarette) from the past? Why this memory? Why now? Because, of course, it is Willie, not Natalie Wood but Willie whom they are reading about in the papers, Willie himself whom the strangers are crying for this time.

How his great lying-in-state would have pleased him! If the dead are in any way allowed to return and witness such things, Willie was there and eavesdropping on his mourners, reveling in the event, like Huckleberry Finn at his own funeral. I am so confident of the ability of that dear great soul of his to continue after death (for if Willie doesn't rise again, no one will) that—now that the flowers are browning on his grave—what I strangely find myself worrying about most are the whereabouts of Skip and Pete. (This, too, was a concern of Willie's; his friends will remember his insistence upon giving Pete a proper burial in the Oxford cemetery.) Buddhist theology gives hope upon this question, as does the theology of my own Roman Catholic faith, but still I return night after night to my heaviest books in an attempt to reassure myself on this point. I don't care how nice Heaven is, really I don't: he's not going to be happy if those dogs aren't there.

And, as I read over these pages (written hastily, as the magazine [*Oxford American*] goes to press), I wonder if I ought to tone down the emotion of these recollections, but no: I absolutely refuse. Willie flung around words like *great* and *noble* and *brave* and *genius* wherever he went—great profligate showers of outdated coin, moidores, guineas, pieces of eight, stamped with all the crowns and statesmen of history. And this is the very coin that I wish to heap up in heavy glittering masses on his grave: "Now cracks a noble heart." He deserves all the glory we are able to give him—the flights of angels singing him to his rest, all of it—for he felt this way about the people and the things that he loved, and it is only natural that we who loved him should wish to bring him the same tribute now that he is gone.

CHRIS THOMPSON

It was a Thursday night after a junior high football game. When I walked inside the house, my mom was standing at the kitchen counter crying. Her eyes and face were red with pain. She tried her best to explain the news of my grandmother's stroke. She tried her best to make it not sound as bad as it was. But her tears told me how bad it was.

Five years ago yesterday, we buried my grandmother. She never fully recovered from the stroke that changed all of our lives in my seventh-grade year. As we made the long drive to Yazoo City that night after the football game, I knew my life had changed. I knew I wasn't a kid anymore.

The years before my grandmother's stroke were good years. She never struggled to talk or move. She never struggled to sit up in her bed. She was vibrant and full of life. She overflowed with gentle warmth and happiness. Her eyes, face, and mouth always smiled. She was the queen of southern grandmotherliness. She would sit patiently in her rocking chair and let my cousins brush and play with her cotton white hair. She loved to cook and garden; she loved to fix me Kool-Aid.

During those good years, when we went to visit my grandparents, each morning brought a day filled with new and simple pleasures. I would spend hours roaming the nearby fields adjacent to their Yazoo County farm. I would climb trees until dark. After supper, I would chase lightning bugs until somebody called me inside. I was a child, and I relished every second.

But after the stroke, the visits were different. They were difficult. I found myself sitting in hospital waiting rooms. I experienced the tragedy of a small, rural nursing home. When I walked the fields, I wasn't playing; I was thinking—trying to understand time and change and the pain of growing up.

The one person who helped me cope with change and growing up more than any other was a kind, talented Yazoo City native by the name of Willie Morris. His writing reminded me of the easy times, and I figured if this guy could make it, I could, too.

The Disney Channel made one of his books into a movie. Maybe some of you have seen the movie *Good Old Boy*. When I was a kid, I must have watched the movie at least twelve times. In my mind, I can picture almost every scene of the movie. I remember Spit McGee and Willie and, of course, the famed Witch of Yazoo. Willie's grandfather, who looked like Mark Twain, always made me laugh.

In high school, I started dating a girl whose dad looked like Mark Twain. He was funny like the grandfather in *Good Old Boy*. I admired and respected him more than he'll probably ever know. A few months into the courtship, I realized my parents didn't like him and that they also didn't approve of my dating his daughter. As more time passed, I also learned that my girlfriend's father, the jovial Mark Twain look-alike, didn't like me or my family. It was another painful change—in some ways, almost as painful as my grandmother's stroke.

Again, Willie Morris came to my aid. The memories of *Good Old Boy* sustained me. In my mind, I could occasionally pretend that the problems of real life didn't exist; his writing could somehow help me intertwine the happy, simpler memories of childhood into a fictitious present. Maybe it wasn't the best way to deal with things, but it helped me to hang on.

On my first day at Ole Miss, I walked downtown to Square Books. I climbed the stairs to the Mississippi writers section. I found a copy of *Good Old Boy* and sat down in a nearby chair to pay tribute to my friend (even though I had never met him, I considered him a friend) and favorite writer.

I opened the book to a passage about baseball—my favorite sport in junior high. Soon Morris's thoughts had my eyes warm and cloudy. I didn't want to cry in public, so I walked downstairs to buy the book and waited until the next day to finish reading it.

A few months later, Willie Morris came to town for a book reading. He read from his latest book, *The Ghosts of Medgar Evers*—a deeply moving work about the making of a movie about the trial of Byron De La Beckwith. After he finished reading, I waited in line for him to sign my copy of *Good Old Boy* and a copy of *My Dog Skip* that my girlfriend had given me for my birthday.

As he signed *Good Old Boy*, I told him that my grandparents had lived in Yazoo and that he was my favorite writer. He asked me what part of the county my grandparents lived in. When I told him "about halfway between Benton and Bentonia," he paused and said that he had just taken Eudora Welty riding through that area on the day before.

When I walked out of the store, I opened the book to look at his signature. In *My Dog Skip*, he wrote, "To Chris, Very best wishes—with Yazoo connections, Willie Morris."

I could tell you more stories about why I love Willie Morris. I could tell you about going down to Jackson to see the driveway where Byron De La Beckwith shot and killed Medgar Evers after reading *The Ghosts of Medgar Evers*. I could tell you about meeting Morris's son David at a blues festival in Canton. But those would take too much space and time.

Instead, I will try to make it simple: I love Willie Morris, because he is the greatest Mississippian who has ever lived; his writing has taught me to love and appreciate the joy and pain of my home state in ways that no other human being could explain. His writings have sustained me during some of my life's hardest and most tragic periods.

Just the other day, I found a book titled *A Century of Heroes.* It's a collection of stories about the first one hundred years of Ole Miss football. Willie Morris contributed several of the stories. I read one about his first trip to an Ole Miss football game. He was in the second grade, and the year was 1941. We beat Arkansas in the rain at Crump Stadium in Memphis; the score was 18–0. Here's a small sample of what he wrote:

> I only recall the cluster of girls in white boots and rain-caps sitting down the way, the boisterous strangers next to me passing a bottle among themselves and drinking from it in long gulps, the sounds of the band and the yells of "Hotty Toddy!", the laughter when one of the men in striped shirts was run over by a player and skidded for yards in the mud, the jubilant chant of "Hovious! Hovious!" when the little silhouette abruptly moved and darted through the other phantoms trying to wrestle him to the earth—and, all about me as I gazed behind me to see if I could find my father, the eternal Southern rain.

Good-bye, Willie. We will miss you.

BILLY WATKINS

Just this week, Willie Morris was to begin a new book.

It would be called "One for My Daddy," about how his father taught him to play and appreciate baseball.

"He was really excited about it," said Jack Bales, who is writing a literary biography of the Mississippi author.

The story will go untold. Morris died Monday night of a heart attack. He was sixty-four.

"There's a blanket of sadness across the whole state," said David Sansing, historian at the University of Mississippi and a longtime friend of Morris's. "Everybody I've talked to says and realizes that we've lost somebody very special to us."

Special in a way that will only magnify as time goes on, said Richard Howorth, owner of Square Books in Oxford.

"Willie was Mississippi's voice," Howorth said. "He spoke for us and about us, and I think he was uniquely able to do that.

"It wasn't that he simply had a greater love of Mississippi or the South than others, although he had a deep love for both. It was more because of his knowledge about history and humanity in general. Because of his perspective, he was able to write about it and help us understand it better."

As former Miss America Mary Ann Mobley, who grew up in Brandon, put it: "Willie loved the South, and he loved Mississippi, and he wrote about us with love—warts and all."

President Clinton said in a statement released Tuesday: "He had an enormous pride in and love for the South, but he also had a passion to right the wrongs of our racial history."

"Despite all his success, Mr. Morris remained tied to his roots by living here in Jackson," said Jackson Mayor Harvey Johnson, Jr. "We have truly lost a native son, an ambassador."

Morris educated the world about his hometown of Yazoo City and his home state with such books as *Good Old Boy*, *My Dog Skip*, and *North Toward Home*.

He also educated Mississippi in unique ways, said John Evans, owner of Lemuria Bookstore in Jackson. "He would bring writers like George Plimpton and William Styron to Lemuria and Square Books, and say, 'Gentlemen, this is your Mississippi home. This is where your stories live while they're here,'" Evans said. "When he brought people like that here, it totally stimulated the cultural environment. He was our connection to such writers."

Evans said Morris's passion to write good stories was equaled only by his determination to help young Mississippi writers.

"Whether it was journalists or blues writers or whatever, Willie was supportive of anyone who was involved in creative aspects," Evans said.

Sansing agreed: "He inspired people. He made people believe in themselves. And the good deeds of Willie Morris are like the proverbial stone cast upon the pond—its ripples will go on forever. He touched a whole lot of people."

One of them was John Grisham, the best-selling novelist and former member of the Mississippi Legislature.

"I didn't really approach him until *A Time to Kill* [Grisham's first book] was done, and I had an agent in New York who wanted to represent me," Grisham said. "I didn't know anybody in New York, not a soul in the publishing world. It was very scary. But Willie knew everybody. We had a very long dinner, talked about it. He made a few phone calls and assured me I was on the right track."

Another was Bales, a reference librarian at Mary Washington College in Fredericksburg, Virginia, who struck up a friendship with Morris simply by writing him a letter.

"I'd read *My Dog Skip* and just loved it," Bales recalled. "He gets thousands of letters—I know because I've been through them all working on the biography—but he took the time to write me back."

Bales and Morris corresponded for weeks. Morris invited Bales to Jackson for a party celebrating the movie *Ghosts of Mississippi* and his book that would be written about it.

"I'm in the hotel there in Jackson and the phone rings," Bales said. "It was Willie. He said, 'Jack, why don't me and you go on a tour of Yazoo City.' He spent the entire day showing me the haunts of his boyhood. He had so much on his plate at that time, but he took so much time with me. And from what others have told me he was that way with a lot of people."

Said Sansing, "They used to say this about [Franklin] Roosevelt, but it was true about Willie, too. When you were in his presence, you felt completely confident that you were his best friend. He inspired you, uplifted you, made you feel better. That's a remarkable trait."

LINTON WEEKS

On the way to see Willie Morris in Oxford, Mississippi, one night in the mid-1980s, we stopped at a small liquor store and bought a big old bottle of Valpolicella. Over dinner, we told Willie what we had in mind. We wanted to start a publication called *Southern Magazine*, a monthly exploration of the region's complexities.

Willie, who knew a lot about magazines and a lot more about the South, opened up his mind and his heart. He reached for the sack the bottle was in and enthusiastically began to sketch out ideas before our very eyes.

"Does the South still exist?" he asked in his soft, mellifluous, rhetorical way. "That's what your first issue should be about: Is there still a South?"

On the brown paper bag he jotted down names of writers we should enlist, good friends of his, folks who would help us wrestle with the notion. The list was a Who's Who of contemporary southern literature.

Willie Morris knew the answer to his own question full well. Of course there is a South. When he died Monday in Jackson, Mississippi, at the age of sixty-four, he took some of that South with him. But what he left behind is a region and a world made lovelier by his talents and largess.

"He had one of the biggest hearts," said Sid Graves, founder of the Delta Blues Museum in Clarksdale, Mississippi. Graves knew and admired Willie for years. Paraphrasing Tennessee Williams, he said that Willie's heart "was as big as a football."

"He had an extraordinarily keen mind for literature and

ideas. I liked to hear him talk about football," recalled Chicago poet and professor Sterling Plumpp. "There was a kind of generosity in Willie Morris that I liked."

"I was always struck," said William Ferris, chairman of the National Endowment for the Humanities and former head of the Center for the Study of Southern Culture at the University of Mississippi, "by his devotion to friends. His relationships with writers like William Styron, James Dickey, Ralph Ellison, and Robert Penn Warren were deep and significant friendships. Many of these writers came to Oxford to honor Willie."

Willie honored Oxford by moving there in 1980 to become writer-in-residence at the University of Mississippi. Born in Jackson in 1934, Willie grew up in Yazoo City (pop. 7,000), a place he immortalized in several of his books, including *Yazoo* and *North Toward Home*. He gloried in small-town life— baseball games, dogs, playing taps for military funerals. He went to the University of Texas on a baseball scholarship and was editor of the campus newspaper, then attended the other Oxford as a Rhodes Scholar. He married Celia Buchan from Houston. They had a son, David Rae, in England. Under Britain's health plan, Willie told his friends, his son's birth cost him eighty-seven cents. The couple eventually divorced.

In Europe, Willie traveled with fellow Rhodes Scholar Edwin Yoder. Yesterday, Yoder, who lives in Alexandria, recalled their many escapades, including the time Willie, on a lark, dangled from the bridge at Avignon.

After England, Willie returned to Austin as editor of the *Texas Observer*.

Playwright Larry L. King met Willie at the *Observer*, and they became lifelong buds. In fact, almost everyone who met Willie became a friend for life. "I never knew Willie to do anybody harm or to want to," King said yesterday. "He was a helpful fellow to writers. That's unusual in this business."

In 1963, Willie went to work for *Harper's* magazine; he was named editor in 1967 and resigned in 1971. He opened the magazine up to new writers and longer pieces, said David Halberstam, a contributor to the magazine (and whose profile there of McGeorge Bundy became the seed of *The Best and the Brightest*).

Willie had a mischievous mind. When Halberstam's book was near the top of the bestseller list, he received a phone call one day from a man who said he had written a diet guide that was also very high on the list. "Perhaps we could collaborate on a book that would have stunning success," the man said to Halberstam, who realized about this time that the caller was Willie. "We could call it 'The Best and the Fattest.'"

"Willie had the lowest index of malice of anybody I ever met," Halberstam said. "That probably worked against him as he got up higher in the world of publishing."

He added: "He was not a great infighter. I don't think he was great at protecting his flank. There was part of him that was like a little boy."

In 1976, Willie spent some time here as writer-in-residence at the *Washington Star*.

Though he continued to write for a few years in Bridgehampton, New York, and loiter with the literati—James Jones, Truman Capote, Irwin Shaw—he longed to see cotton fields instead of potato fields. In 1980, he moved back to Mississippi for good. He chose Oxford, a college town with palpable literary history. One of his best friends there was Dean Faulkner Wells, the niece of William Faulkner, another Oxford favorite son.

Yesterday morning Dean and her husband, Larry Wells, were sitting at their kitchen table, grieving over the loss of their longtime friend and turning to Willie's writing and other literature for solace. "Larry and I were looking for the words Willie loved the most," Dean said, fighting back tears. They read the poetry of Wallace Stevens and A. E. Housman.

"He really took care of the people he loved," she said.

Oxford, circa 1980, was an exciting swirl of literary activity. Ferris established the Center for the Study of Southern Culture. Richard Howorth opened his legendary bookstore. Larry and Dean Wells owned Yoknapatawpha Press, which published Willie's books and reprinted some of Faulkner's.

"It was a great time," Larry Wells recalled. "Willie always said, 'I came home, and it was not too late.'"

In Mississippi, Willie gave guidance to young writers in the classroom and out. And he wrote new books, including *The Courting of Marcus Dupree*, about an outstanding football player; *My Dog Skip*, which was made into a movie; *Terrains of the Heart*, a collection of essays; and a number of art books including *Homecomings*, a collaboration with Mississippi painter Bill Dunlap [who now lives in McLean].

Yesterday Dunlap was remembering all that Willie meant to him and other expatriate southerners. "He took a bridge out of Mississippi," Dunlap said, "then he took that bridge and came back."

To celebrate the publication of *Homecomings*, Sen. Thad Cochran (R-Miss.) threw a big bash on Capitol Hill for Willie and Dunlap in the late 1980s. The painter stood up and said a few words. Willie climbed on a table and announced that he was marrying the book's editor, JoAnne Prichard.

She was the one who answered his cry when he collapsed Monday afternoon at his writing table at their home in Jackson. He died in the evening of heart failure.

So, does the South still exist? True to his word, in the first issue of *Southern Magazine*, which appeared in October 1986, Willie Morris addressed head-on the question he raised along with a glass of red wine on that long, heady night in Oxford. In the answering, he also spoke of the way he chose to live his own life.

"One has to seek the answer on one's own terms, of course, but to do that I suggest one should spurn the boardrooms and the country clubs and the countless college seminars on the subject and spend a little time at the ball games and the funerals and the bus stations and the courthouses and the bargain-rate beauty parlors and the little churches and the roadhouses and the joints near closing hour. . . .

"Perhaps in the end it is the old devil-may-care instinct of the South that remains in the most abundance and will sustain the South in its uncertain future," he wrote. "It is gambling with the heart. It is a glass menagerie. It is something that won't let go."

EDWIN M. YODER, JR.

Willie Morris, the Mississippi writer and editor, died unexpectedly of heart failure at St. Dominic's Hospital in his native city of Jackson on August 2. He and his wife, JoAnne Prichard, had just returned from a happy trip to New York City for a private screening of the movie based on Willie's book, *My Dog Skip.*

Risking cliché, which had no foothold in Willie's richly original world, it could be said that nothing defined his life quite so clearly as the leaving of it. Two days after his death he became only the third Mississippian in this century to lie in state under the dome of the Old Capitol building in Jackson. [See William Faulkner's *Requiem for a Nun* for an interesting evocation of the structure's historic significance.] Hundreds paid their respects. Then some three dozen of Willie's friends adjourned to a nearby beanery whose cheerfully seedy decor and crepuscular lighting recalled those many hangouts Willie had graced over the years, from the front parlor of the King's Arms in Oxford to that nondescript Chinese place on Park Avenue South where he transacted business during his editorship of *Harper's* magazine, to Bobby Vann's bar in Bridgehampton. Later that afternoon, the cortege proceeded to the First Methodist Church of Yazoo City, the small town where he had grown up on the edge of the great Mississippi Delta.

William Styron and others paid eloquent tribute and the presiding parson, Will Campbell, a hero of the civil rights movement in its stormy days, brought the house down when he called for a standing ovation. Finally, exactly 13 steps from the famous witch's grave in the old Yazoo cemetery, Willie was laid to rest to the sound of taps, as he had played it as a youthful trumpeter for the Korean War dead.

One begins the story with its ending for good reason; but first, perhaps his obituarist may be permitted a personal impression or two; for we had been the best of friends for more than forty-three years—even before destiny put us on the same boat to Oxford in early October 1956. As fellow college editors in the preceding academic year, we had both landed in hot water—his far hotter than mine, for in *Daily Texan* editorials he had questioned the sanctity of the oil depletion allowance: heresy of heresies in Texas—and had formed, by correspondence, a sort of mutual support association.

As a writer, Willie Morris was a rare combination of artistry with penetrating intellect. Behind the sometimes drowsy or passive-seeming exterior, he was a polymath who knew a great deal about a great many important things, especially American and southern history and literature. He had that most invaluable of the writer's devices, famously described by Ernest Hemingway as a reliable shinola-detector (Hemingway used a stronger word); and in my view Willie Morris was the best reporter of his age on the texture of the turbulent southern experience in this century.

As a man, Willie was without detectable vanity or egotism. He was a wonderful listener, missing nothing, recalling everything, with an exquisitely sensitive emotional register. Once when he and Jane and I were sitting late at Elaine's, the New York literary cafe at which he was a fixture, he and Jane began talking about Scott Fitzgerald's novel *Tender Is the Night*; and that led to a discussion of the tragedy of Scott and Zelda: a recollection that so upset Willie he left Elaine's to walk around the block for half an hour.

When we traveled all over Europe together, he carried his clothes and books in a worn suitcase without a handle, which he would hoist and carry on his shoulder. It was heavy, too, because we all lugged heavy tomes with us on these hegiras, in the usually vain hope of intervals of study between the cathedrals and the bull fights. When we traveled together I always took extra money along because Willie had no idea how much he would need and usually ran short. He always repaid debts promptly—he was a man with a most acute sense of personal honor. His reading glasses were missing one rim for God knows how long, a year or more, after which the new-found rim would be attached with adhesive tape for a while. In later life, he came to hate ringing telephones and often shut his in the refrigerator, which muted its ringing. You had to know an elaborate dialing code to get through to him; and even that was chancy. Willie never cared about clothes, so far as I knew, or shoes either. Even on formal occasions, I never saw him in a pair of pants that weren't a bit baggy. He preferred ratty old pullover sweaters to jackets and ties; he was no fashion plate. A discerning friend said of him when he died: "Among superbly creative people, who usually have big and sometimes unmanageable egos, he was the freest from petty neurosis and self-absorption of anyone I have known. He had no defenses and needed none."

Not the least of reasons for beginning Willie's story with its ending was that he had followed Dr. Freud's advice and had made friends with death. The friendship took the form of a passionate interest in cemeteries. He had prowled every notable burying ground from Oxford to Hollywood, from Boston to New Orleans—not in a spirit of morbidity but because their quiet precincts, the resting place of "the great silent majority," as Willie called the departed, offered a prism into the human comedy. There, past merged with present in that incremental narrative of people and events, past and present, that constituted Willie's unique slant on the world. There was, of course, a hint of the wise old counsel, memento mori, in this. He wrote of this early affection in a poignant passage in *North Toward Home*: "The cemetery [he said of the place where he now lies] held no horror for me. It was set on a beautiful wooded hill overlooking the whole town. I loved to walk among the graves and look at the dates and words on the tombstones. I learned more about the town's past here, the migrations, the epidemics, the old forgotten tragedies, than I could ever have learned in the library."

Yet no one was ever less defined, or preoccupied, by death. Willie was an antic spirit, centrally animated at his core by the soul of the mischievous ten-year-old boy he had been. He loved to play jokes and pranks on his friends, most of them amusing and benevolent. It could have surprised no one who knew him that his last known dream involved the amusing sabotage of a fancy dinner party at the Martha's Vineyard summer place of his friend Bill Styron. There was, as I have good reason to know, a beguiling charm in Willie's jokes and tricks that almost made one want to be fooled; that is why his friends so often were. Once as we were being driven through the kudzu-shrouded woodlands of north Mississippi, Willie persuaded me that the man who had imported the now un-controlled anti-erosion ground cover plant to the U.S. was still alive, in Oxford, Mississippi. When I asked if I might be able to interview him, Willie said that the man was so mortified by the vine's fecund rampancy that he had become a hermit and withdrawn from all human society. When I naively re-ported the story in my newspaper column, a southern editor I knew was on the phone within minutes.

"What is this s— about kudzu?" Claude Sitton demanded.

"S—?" I asked. "What do you mean, Claude?"

"If the man who imported kudzu is still living, he's 158 years old."

Claude knew; he had once written about the menace of the plant for *The New York Times*.

Willie once convinced my daughter Anne (aged twelve) during an after-dinner walk on Long Island that if she listened very carefully at dusk, she could hear the ghost of John Philip Sousa playing his horn on the front porch of his summer cottage: a dark house up a long tree-lined lane. With that uncanny circumstantial improvisation that his friends knew so well, Willie added that the composer of "The Stars and Stripes Forever," and other great marches, had come to this country as an Italian immigrant boy named John Phillipe. He was so proud of being a new American, Willie said, that he signed his semi-literate postcards back to the old country, "John Phillipe, USA," soon elided to John Philip Sousa! Who could doubt it?

If life for Willie was a narrative, growing with experience like the rings of a great oak, and compounded not only of his deep learning in history and letters but of his fabulous memory for old scenes and talk, one striking ingredient was a skein of fables whose quota of truthfulness was hard to fix. Memories of these fables flowed nonstop during those sad early August days in Jackson, as his friends sought to measure the vacancy his death had left behind. In his funeral tribute, David Halberstam, whose talents as a chronicler of American life Willie was among the first to recognize and display in the pages of *Harper's*, recalled a typical tale. When Halberstam's best-selling book, *The Best and the Brightest*, was bumped by a diet book from the top of the *New York Times* list, he had a call from Willie, affecting a donnish voice and speaking as the supposed author of the diet book. The diet "doctor" apologized to Halberstam but then proposed a future collaboration that would make them both rich. "I even have a title," he said. "We will call it 'The Best and the Fattest.'"

From a thick album of similar antics, I recall the night in the fall of 1957 when Willie telephoned the Royal Humane Society offices in London from our digs at 22 St. Margaret's Road. Speaking in broken English for the wholly fictitious "Oxford East European Society," Willie lodged a protest against the propulsion of the dog Laika into space by a Russian sputnik. "Do ze Roshian parparians haf any vey of gettink this poor creature back to ze eardt?" he asked the puzzled but sympathetic lady at the other end of the line. When the same whimsical mood came over him, Willie would suddenly lean forward in those boxy London taxis and loudly address the bewildered driver: "Roshian people do not vant var," he would bellow through the glass partition. "Only crazy Amerikanskis vant var. Do Ainglish beople vant var? Do not hang out vith varmonger Amerikanskis."

Willie's tireless flow of nonsense was a big part of him, obviously, for indeed he did view life as fundamentally comic; but it was only a part and perhaps the lesser part, after all. He was otherwise a deeply serious man, chastened and deepened by the experience of a sensitive childhood in race-obsessed Mississippi. His distinctions, literary and civic, to say nothing of his good works, would require many pages to list. But three paramount accomplishments may perhaps be approximated here briefly.

He did more than any Mississippian of his generation to recall his troubled state from the brink of political terrorism, to hearten its better angels and to coax it towards the vibrant racial goodwill that prevails there today. His return from two decades of exile to Mississippi in 1980, to be writer-in-residence at Ole Miss, was an effort of will and integration. As he wrote in *New York Days*: "Here I was back again in the sweet and deep dark womb of home. The eternal juxtaposition of . . . hate and love, the apposition of its severity and tenderness, would forever baffle and enrage me . . . but these forever drive me to words. Meanness is everywhere, but here the meanness and the desperation and the nobility have for me their own dramatic edge, for the fools are my fools, and the heroes are mine too." The theme of redemption and reconciliation in a troubled but beloved society figured in two fine books: *Yazoo*, about the belated integration of schools in his hometown; and *The Courting of Marcus Dupree*, in which he explored the ironies of interracial amity in Philadelphia, Mississippi, a bare generation after even the law enforcement officials of "bloody Neshoba" had colluded in the unspeakable assassination of three young civil rights workers.

During his tenure as associate editor, then editor-in-chief of *Harper's* (1963-71), he transformed a sedate magazine into the most vital and admired forum in the country for fine writing on great matters at a time of national troubles. His recruitment of writers was spectacular. Norman Mailer's memorable history-as-novel, "The Steps of the Pentagon," was a Willie Morris production, delivered at 100,000 words, all of which were run in a single issue of the magazine. As were Styron's "This Quiet Dust," a prose overture to his great novel about the Nat Turner slave rebellion, and David Halberstam's searing profiles of the "best and the brightest" who had blundered into the Vietnam calamity. Willie was an editor of boldness and imagination, cut from the same rare mold as Harold Ross of the original *New Yorker* and the unsung Britton Hadden, the creative spirit behind the early *Time* magazine. But his administrative methods were unorthodox and sometimes disorderly from the point of view of his owners, and his more or less forced resignation as editor in 1971 brought down a brilliant regime; and great was the fall thereof. When Jane and I and our children spent a week with him shortly afterward, when he was living in Muriel O. Murphy's great house on Georgica Pond in the Hamptons and saturating himself nightly in Mahalia Jackson gospel songs and a recorded recitation of General Lee's farewell to his troops, I saw several huge boxes of correspondence, all unopened, all probably tributes to his fallen editorship. I offered to help sort them; Willie was content to ignore them, and I wonder if he ever read them.

Finally, but not least, Willie's precocious autobiography *North Toward Home* will surely live after him as one of the immortal American self-portraits, with those of Mark Twain,

Henry Adams, and John A. Rice. (Rice, a South Carolina Rhodes Scholar of an earlier vintage, wrote a delightful memoir called *I Came Out of the Eighteenth Century*, which I had the pleasure of recommending to Willie. Out of the ether late one night came a distressed phone call from New York. Willie had loved the book and as was his custom had tried to phone Rice to say so. "But Yoder," he said, in a tone of despair, "he's dead.")

Those who were not only friends but writers also knew that Willie watched over them and their work from any distance, like a literary guardian angel. He poured great energy into matching writers with their proper subjects and destinies: destinies which he often saw more clearly and quickly than they. In Jackson on the day of his burial, my old Chapel Hill friend Eli Evans said, "Willie changed my life." It was Willie, then editor of *Harper's*, who suggested to Eli one day at lunch that he could and should write fine books about the peculiar experience of southern Jewry. That suggestion led to a distinguished book called *The Provincials: A Personal History of Jews in the South*, recently reissued with a Willie Morris introduction by Free Press as part of its own fiftieth anniversary celebration; and a few years later to a widely-praised biography of Judah P. Benjamin, the Confederate secretary of state. Two of my own books were published in Mississippi, largely through his patronage; and ours—Eli's and mine—are merely representative cases, among scores of hundreds. A large and significant part of the journalism of the 1960s and early 1970s bore Willie's imprimatur in some form. He had planted the seed, or edited a manuscript, or conceptualized an as yet unarticulated book, or encouraged reluctant writers to mine their hidden strengths.

With all the rest, Willie was a gregarious creature with a gift for mimicry and entertainment. It accounted in part for the acolytes who gathered around any table or event, wherever he perched. That gift rested on a verbal edge whose subtlety sometimes emerged with years, like the bouquet of a fine wine. Thus the grandsons of John Hancock, improbably buried in Yazoo City, had died of "some colorful disease." The impersonal funerals Willie witnessed in New York told a bleak tale of the loneliness of "natural death." Perhaps you needn't be a writer to sense the genius of those exacting adjectives, "colorful" or "natural," but the fact is that Willie's sense of words was pristine. He had the artist's capacity for seeing it new. It was Willie, contemplating a gray day in Oxford not long after we came there, who said: "O to be in April, now that England's here." Having coined this enviable *bon mot*, he gave it away *gratis*, generously attributing it to Jess Woods, a classmate who had died just after returning from England. When he answered my call to speak to this or that group in North Carolina, he would say: "I'm going to attack the Red Chinese." After he had digested the tangled royal genealogies of Anglo-Saxon England, he described any fatuous reactionary as being "to the right of Ethelred the Unready," a great improvement on the hackneyed Genghis Khan. He loved to point out that his son David, born on the National Health Scheme in Oxford, "cost eighty-seven cents." Of the Confederacy and the event of our Civil War, he said (in fun, I hope I needn't add, but still with a southerner's edge): "We had the greatest armies ever put in the field, but our machines failed us."

Willie's observant obituarist in *The New York Times* of August 3, Peter Applebome, wrote with unusual candor of Willie's notorious indifference to the rules of good health: "Mr. Morris drank too much bourbon and red wine, smoked too many Viceroys, stayed up too late and caroused too much." It was true. When his classmates of 1956 first met him when the *Flandre* sailed from New York in October 1956, Willie was a lithe, athletic and fresh-faced boy, an accomplished athlete who had gone to Texas on a baseball scholarship. But sometime in his late twenties or thereabouts, Willie, a born night-owl in any case, had turned his back on the life of fitness for wine, women, and song and never looked back: not a bad swap, perhaps, for an artist. Willie's excesses became for a time a matter of concern and alarm among his old friends. At times, it was as if Willie wished to be numbered with the many great American writers, Thomas Wolfe and Fitzgerald and others, who had lived at the outer edge and paid a price for doing so. "They say I have a bourbon problem," Willie remarked to Jane and me one night, in one of his more reckless moods. "Hell, I don't have a problem. I can get all the bourbon I want."

Then good fortune brought the lovely and distinguished JoAnne Prichard into his life. She too had lived in Yazoo City and was a fellow editor as well; and most of all she understood and valued him for his unmatched kindness and originality. There followed a final decade's renaissance of fine writing and new accomplishment, including a mounting interest in movies and their making, as chronicled in his book about the making of a film about the civil rights martyr Medgar Evers, *Ghosts of Mississippi*, for which he had written the original treatment. But alas, no one could altogether undo the wear and tear of the years.

His loving friends had been forced to realize, long since, that there was in Willie's temperament some unfathomable strain of the incurable wound that strengthens and directs the magic bow of art, even as in Edmund Wilson's memorable essay. The wound and the bow were intricately fused, as they often are in those of comic genius. Stunned and grieved as we were by his sudden departure, with his big book on baseball just begun, I believe that his friends would agree on one thing: If it was only by living his life at so costly a pitch of intensity that this rare spirit might teach and delight us, the cost was well repaid, every penny of it.

A Love That Transcends Sadness

BY WILLIE MORRIS

Not too long ago, in a small Southern town where I live, I was invited by friends to go with them and their children to the cemetery to help choose their burial plot. My friends are in the heartiest prime of life and do not anticipate departing the Lord's earth immediately, and hence, far from being funereal, our search had an adventurous mood to it, like picking out a Christmas tree. It was that hour before twilight, and the marvelous old graveyard with its cedars and magnolias and flowering glades sang with the Mississippi springtime. The honeysuckled air was an affirmation of the tugs and tremors of living. My companions had spent all their lives in the town, and the names on even the oldest stones were as familiar to them as the people they saw every day. "Location," the man of the family said, laughing, "As the real-estate magnates say, we want *location.*"

At last they found a plot in the most venerable section which was to their liking, having spurned a shady spot which I had recommended under a giant oak. I knew the caretaker would soon have to come to this place of their choice with a long, thin steel rod, shoving it into the ground every few inches to see if it struck forgotten coffins. If not, this plot was theirs. Our quest had been a tentative success, and we retired elsewhere to celebrate.

Their humor coincided with mine, for I am no stranger to graveyards. With rare exceptions, ever since my childhood, they have suffused me not with foreboding but with a sense of belonging and, as I grow older, with a curious, ineffable tenderness. My dog Pete and I go out into the cemeteries not only to escape the telephone, and those living beings who place more demands on us than the dead ever would, but to feel a continuity with the flow of the generations. "Living," William Faulkner wrote, "is a process of getting ready to be dead for a long time."

I have never been lonely in a cemetery. They are perfect places to observe the slow changing of the seasons, and to absorb human history—the tragedies and anguishes, the violences and treacheries, and always the guilts and sorrows of vanished people. In a preternatural quiet, one can almost hear the palpable, long-ago voices.

I like especially the small-town cemeteries of America where the children come for picnics and games, as we did when I was growing up—wandering among the stones on our own, with no adults about, to regard the mystery and inevitability of death, on its terms and ours. I remember we would watch the funerals from afar in a hushed awe, and I believe that was when I became obsessed not with death itself but with the singular community of death and life together—and life's secrets, life's fears, life's surprises. Later, in high school, as I waited on a hill to play the echo to taps on my trumpet for the Korean War dead, the tableau below with its shining black hearse and the coffin enshrouded with the flag and the gathering mourners was like a folk drama, with the earth as its stage.

The great urban cemeteries of New York City always filled me with horror, the mile after mile of crowded tombstones which no one ever seemed to visit, as if one could *find* anyone in there even if he wished to. Likewise, the suburban cemeteries of this generation with their carefully manicured lawns and bronze plaques embedded in the ground, all imbued with affluence and artifice, are much too remote for me. My favorites have always been in the old, established places where people honor the long dead and the new graves are in proximity with the most ancient. The churchyard cemeteries of England haunted me with the eternal rhythms of time. In one of these, years ago as a student at Oxford, I found this inscription:

> *Here lies Johnny Kongapod,*
> *Have mercy on him, gracious God,*
> *As he would on You if he was God,*
> *And You were Johnny Kongapod*

Equally magnetic were the graveyards of eastern Long Island, with their patina of the past touched ever so mellowly with the present. The cemetery of Wainscot, Long Island, only a few hundred yards from the Atlantic Ocean, surrounded the schoolhouse. I would watch the children playing at recess among the graves. Later I discovered a man and his wife juxtaposed under identical stones. On the wife's tomb was "Rest in Peace." On the man's, at the same level, was "No Comment." I admired the audacity of that.

But it is the graveyards of Mississippi which are the most moving for me, having to do, I believe, with my belonging here. They spring from the earth itself, and beckon me time and again. The crumbling stones of my people evoke in me the terrible enigmas of living. In a small Civil War cemetery which I came across recently, the markers stretching away in a misty haze, it occurred to me that most of these boys had never even had a girlfriend. I have found a remote graveyard in the hills with photographs on many of the stones, some nearly one hundred years old, the women in bonnets and Sunday dresses, the men in overalls—"the short and simple annals of the poor." I am drawn here to the tiny grave of a little girl. Her name was Fairy Jumper, and she lived from April 14, 1914, to January 16, 1919. There is a miniature lamb at the top of the stone, and the words: "A fairer bud of promise never bloomed." There are no other Jumpers around her, and there she is, my Fairy, in a far corner of that country burial ground, so forlorn and alone that it is difficult to bear. It was in this cemetery on a bleak February noon that I caught sight of four men digging a grave in the hard, unyielding soil. After a time they gave up. After they left, a man drove toward me in a battered truck. He wanted to know if some fellows had been working on the grave. Yes, I said, but they went away. "Well, I can't finish all by myself." Wordlessly, I helped him dig.

One lonesome, windswept afternoon my dog and I were sitting at the crest of a hill in the town cemetery. Down below us, the acres of empty land were covered with wildflowers. A new road was going in down there, the caretaker had told me; the area was large enough to accommodate the next three generations. "With the economy so bad," I had asked him, "how can you be *expanding*?" He had replied: "It comes in spurts. Not a one last week. Five put down the week before. It's a pretty steady business."

Sitting there now in the dappled sunshine, a middle-aged man and his middle-aged dog, gazing across at the untenanted terrain awaiting its dead, I thought of how each generation lives with its own exclusive solicitudes—the passions, the defeats, the victories, the sacrifices. The names and dates and the faces belong to each generation in its own passing, for much of everything except the most unforgettable is soon forgotten. And yet: though much is taken, much abides. I thought then of human beings, on this cinder of a planet out at the edge of the universe, not knowing where we came from, why we are here, or where we might go after death—and yet we still laugh, and cry, and feel, and love.

"All that we can know about those we have loved and lost," Thornton Wilder wrote, "is that they would wish us to remember them with a more intensified realization of their reality. What is essential does not die but clarifies. The highest tribute to the dead is not grief but gratitude."

FUNERAL EULOGIES

Reverend Will D. Campbell, 5 August 1999. Reprinted by permission of the author.

William Styron, 5 August 1999. Published as "It Cannot Be Long," *Oxford American*, September/October 1999. Reprinted by permission of the author.

David Halberstam, 5 August 1999. Reprinted by permission of the author.

Mike Espy, 5 August 1999. Reprinted by permission of the author.

Josephine Ayres Haxton (Ellen Douglas), 5 August 1999. Reprinted by permission of the author.

Governor William F. Winter, 5 August 1999. Reprinted by permission of the author.

Harriet DeCell Kuykendall, 5 August 1999. Reprinted by permission of the author.

Jill Conner Browne, 5 August 1999. Reprinted by permission of the author.

Winston F. Groom, 5 August 1999. Reprinted by permission of the author.

PUBLISHED TRIBUTES

Peter Applebome, "Obituary: Willie Morris, 64, Writer on the Southern Experience." *The New York Times*, 3 August 1999. Copyright © 1999 by the New York Times Co. Reprinted by permission.

Rick Bragg, "To a Beloved Native Son, a Mississippi Farewell." *The New York Times*, 6 August 1999. Reprinted by permission of the author.

President Bill Clinton, "Eulogy." Published in *Time*, 16 August 1999. Reprinted by permission of the White House.

Raad Cawthon, "Eloquent in Voicing His Roots, Humanity." *Philadelphia Inquirer*, 5 August 1999. Reprinted by permission of the author.

Chad Clanton, "The Magic of Morris: Southern Author Was Able to Speak to the Best Parts of Ourselves." *Austin American-Statesman*, 8 August 1999. Reprinted by permission of the author.

Rick Cleveland, "Willie Really Was a Good Ol' Boy." *The Clarion-Ledger* [Jackson, Miss.], 6 August 1999. Reprinted by permission of the author.

Paul Greenberg, "Goin' Home: On the Death of Willie Morris." *Arkansas Democrat-Gazette*, 4 August 1999. Reprinted by permission of the author.

Orley Hood, "Our Good Old Boy Always Stood Up for His Mississippi." *The Clarion-Ledger* [Jackson, Miss.], 4 August 1999. Reprinted by permission of the author.

Rheta Grimsley Johnson, "In Reality, Willie Morris Turned South Toward Home." *The Atlanta Journal-Constitution*, 8 August 1999. Reprinted by permission of the author.

Deborah Mathis, "Willie Morris: Life Not Always Fair, But He Relished It." 4 August 1999. Copyright © Tribune Media Services, Inc. All Rights Reserved. Reprinted with permission.

Bill Minor, "Some Say Willie Morris Was Mississippi's Second William Faulkner; I Called Him Friend." *The Clarion-Ledger* [Jackson, Miss.], 12 September 1999. Reprinted by permission of the author.

Sid Salter, "Up in 'Willie's Heaven,' Morris Will Be Telling Mississippi Stories That God Will Want to Hear." *The Scott County Times* [Miss.], 4 August 1999. Reprinted by permission of the author.

Michael Skube, "Once a Shining Star at *Harper's*, Troubled Life Ends on Happier Note." *The Atlanta Journal-Constitution*, 4 August 1999. Reprinted by permission of the author.

Donna Tartt, "Willie Morris, 1934-1999." *Oxford American*, September/October 1999. Reprinted by permission of the author.

Chris Thompson, "Farewell to Mississippi's 'Good Ole Boy.'" *The Daily Mississippian* [University of Mississippi, Oxford, Miss.], 3 August 1999. Reprinted by permission of the author.

Billy Watkins, "Willie Morris: A Few Last Words." *The Clarion-Ledger* [Jackson, Miss.], 4 August 1999. Reprinted by permission of the publisher.

Linton Weeks, "Appreciation: Willie Morris, Heart of the South." *The Washington Post*, 4 August 1999. Reprinted by permission of the author.

Edwin M. Yoder, Jr., "Willie Morris: A Personal Memoir." *The American Oxonian*, Autumn 1999. Reprinted with permission from *The American Oxonian*, Autumn 1999.

Willie Morris, "A Love That Transcends Sadness." *Parade*, 13 September 1981. Reprinted by permission of the Estate of Willie Morris.